TEACHING DISABILITY

ACADEMY OF REHABILITATION PSYCHOLOGY SERIES

Series Editors
Bruce Caplan, *Editor-in-Chief*
Timothy Elliott
Janet Farmer
Robert Frank
Barry Nierenberg
George Prigatano
Daniel Rohe
Stephen Wegener

Volumes in the Series

Ethics Field Guide: Applications in Rehabilitation Psychology
Thomas R. Kerkhoff and Stephanie L. Hanson

The Social Psychology of Disability
Dana S. Dunn

Disability-Affirmative Therapy: A Case Formulation Template for Clients With Disabilities
Rhoda Olkin

Validity Assessment in Rehabilitation Psychology and Settings
Dominic A. Carone and Shane S. Bush

Suicide Prevention After Neurodisability: An Evidence-Informed Approach
Grahame K. Simpson and Lisa A. Brenner

Understanding the Experience of Disability: Perspectives From Social and Rehabilitation Psychology
Dana S. Dunn

Disability as Diversity: Developing Cultural Competence
Erin E. Andrews

Teaching Disability: Practical Activities for In Class & Homework
Rhoda Olkin

Teaching Disability

PRACTICAL ACTIVITIES FOR IN CLASS AND HOMEWORK

Rhoda Olkin

OXFORD
UNIVERSITY PRESS

OXFORD
UNIVERSITY PRESS

Oxford University Press is a department of the University of Oxford. It furthers the University's objective of excellence in research, scholarship, and education by publishing worldwide. Oxford is a registered trade mark of Oxford University Press in the UK and certain other countries.

Published in the United States of America by Oxford University Press
198 Madison Avenue, New York, NY 10016, United States of America.

© Oxford University Press 2021

All rights reserved. No part of this publication may be reproduced, stored in a retrieval system, or transmitted, in any form or by any means, without the prior permission in writing of Oxford University Press, or as expressly permitted by law, by license, or under terms agreed with the appropriate reproduction rights organization. Inquiries concerning reproduction outside the scope of the above should be sent to the Rights Department, Oxford University Press, at the address above.

You must not circulate this work in any other form
and you must impose this same condition on any acquirer.

Library of Congress Cataloging-in-Publication Data
Names: Olkin, Rhoda, author.
Title: Teaching disability : practical activities for in class and homework / Rhoda Olkin, Ph.D.
Description: New York : Oxford University Press, 2021. |
Series: Academy of rehab psych series |
Includes bibliographical references and index.
Identifiers: LCCN 2021005592 (print) | LCCN 2021005593 (ebook) |
ISBN 9780190850661 (paperback) | ISBN 9780190850685 (epub) |
ISBN 9780197584231
Subjects: LCSH: Disabilities—Study and teaching (Higher) |
People with disabilities—Study and teaching (Higher) |
People with disabilities—Psychology.
Classification: LCC HV1568.2 .O425 2021 (print) | LCC HV1568.2 (ebook) |
DDC 305.9/080711—dc23
LC record available at https://lccn.loc.gov/2021005592
LC ebook record available at https://lccn.loc.gov/2021005593

DOI: 10.1093/oso/9780190850661.001.0001

9 8 7 6 5 4 3 2 1

Printed by Marquis, Canada

Contents

A Background and Basics

THIS SECTION HAS two chapters but no activities. Although it is possible to skip right to the activities in Part B, I think the material in these two chapters will be helpful in a few ways. The first chapter addresses instructors, including those who may have little or no experience teaching about disability. It is an introduction that covers some basic information that could seem like stumbling blocks to feeling more comfortable with the activities. The language of disability (people with disabilities or disabled people) is one topic. Other topics are about the goals of the activities, who the book is designed for, hidden disabilities, and intersectionality (which is addressed three times throughout the book). It normalizes some degree of bias and trepidation about teaching a topic most instructors know little about. Lastly it makes a case for why you should read chapter 2.

In chapter 2 I cover the core research that informed the activities in this book. I outline the overarching goals for the activities and discuss the bidirectional relationship between attitudes and behaviors and the troubling low correlation between the two. The bases for the predominantly negative attitudes, mostly from social psychology, are presented, and studies on explicit versus implicit bias towards disability are discussed. A summary of changing attitudes toward disability is next, followed by a strong admonition against using simulation exercises to learn about disability with a rationale. All of the references cited follow this chapter. I think chapter 2 will be helpful to ground instructors, but I suggest considering having this chapter be homework reading for students, as it would likewise give them a small research base before doing any of the activities.

1 Introduction for Instructors

THIS BOOK CONTAINS over two dozen possible activities for either in-class exercises or as homework to be used in undergraduate and graduate courses addressing disability as an aspect of diversity. Included for each activity is the rationale or goal, the materials needed, how to use the activities, the likely time frame, talking points, and potential problems and their possible solutions. Any necessary handouts can also be accessed at http://www.rolkin.com.

This first chapter addresses the rationale and goals for this book. In Chapter 2, I provide a review of the research literature related to teaching about disability. Chapters 4 through 8 contain activities that require minimal preparation, have few potential problems, and are adaptable for many courses and scenarios. Chapters 9 and 10 are more advanced activities in terms of goals, time to do the activities, and possible outcomes. Chapter 11 contains possible measures to assess the outcomes of the activities in this book. These measures are based on the literature review in Chapter 2 and are included to encourage outcome research on disability activities as part of teaching graduate students.

Language: In the sixth edition of the *Publication Manual of the American Psychological Association* (APA; 2010), the use of "people-first" language was encouraged. Examples include people with disabilities, a person with schizophrenia, a person with spinal cord injury, and a wheelchair user. However, the seventh edition (APA, 2020) gives the option to use either person-first or identity-first language. With identity-first language, "the disability becomes the focus, which allows

Teaching Disability. Rhoda Olkin, Oxford University Press. © Oxford University Press 2021.
DOI: 10.1093/oso/9780190850661.003.0001

the individual to claim the disability and choose their identity rather than permitting others . . . to name it or to select terms with negative implications" (APA, 2020 p. 136). I use both types of terms in this book but do encourage classroom discussion of the two perspectives and their assumptions and implications. Using the section in the APA style manual on bias-free language (pp. 131–149) allows the discussion to be more broadly based on many different identities rather than solely on disability as a special case.

Who Is This Book for? This book is for instructors of various types of undergraduate and graduate classes. The beginning-level exercises could be used with a wide variety of courses, from art and music to math and engineering. However, the more advanced-level exercises may require some clinical skills (e.g., in interviewing) and thus are more appropriately used with various mental health trainees and professionals. As I am a clinical psychologist, I have developed these activities with my graduate students in clinical psychology in mind as well as counselors, rehabilitation psychologists, school psychologists, marriage and family therapists, and social workers. And there is a very important caveat: Although I argue against using many forms of "disability simulations" as a teaching tool (see review and discussion of simulation exercises in Chapter 2), there are certain professions where putting oneself in the position of a person with a disability is essential. For example, a sighted web designer should try to use the website without vision. A person designing a wheelchair-accessible hotel room would do well to enter and navigate the room in a wheelchair. Architects should try to experience accessibility from many vantage points. These are not so much simulations as beta tests and could readily point to obvious problems (e.g., the foot-operated lamp I encountered in a putatively wheelchair-accessible hotel room).

What Are the Goals of These Activities? The overarching goal is to make the world a more accessible, equitable, and integrated place for all people with various types of impairments. This cannot happen if outsiders (i.e., those without disabilities) fail to understand the true nature of disability experiences. Many able-bodied people believe that the impairment itself is the main cause of disability, whereas those with disabilities will invariably point to the myriad ways in which they are disadvantaged—socially, politically, economically, architecturally—through stigma, prejudice, microaggressions, and discrimination. Thus, many of the activities herein include elements related to these disadvantages. However, even if these disadvantages could be magically erased, the impairment would remain, so some exercises focus on the personal experience of living with a disability (e.g., pain, fatigue).

Why Do Disability-Related Activities? For any disadvantaged minority group, outsiders to that group often misjudge the insider experience. Disability cannot possibly be understood by simulating a disability, as the simulation mimics only a small fraction of the experience of living with a disability (see review of disability simulations in Chapter 2). Therefore, a combination of activities approaches the insider experience from a variety of aspects. The activities are designed to engage the student both intellectually and emotionally and to maximize the possibility of changes in attitudes, emotions, cognitions, beliefs, and behaviors.

What About Intersectionality? Disadvantaged minorities are often the subject of study in isolation, that is, as if the disability characteristic is the defining one and other characteristics are of lesser importance. This has been true for people with disabilities as well. To counter this, some exercises deliberately include issues related not only to disability but also to other stigmatized statuses as well. An overarching talking point in debriefing any of the activities is to raise the issue of intersectionality (e.g., gay men with disabilities) and imagine the activity from varying perspectives. For example, a vignette could be altered to have the person portrayed as inhabiting two or more stigmatized or disadvantages statuses (e.g., a female immigrant from Guatemala with an autoimmune disorder). An observation activity might ask for demographic data about those observed. An interview could be assigned that would be done with a person representing at least two minority statuses. The counter to disadvantage is privilege. Many people embody a combination of the two, having some aspects of disadvantage (e.g., gay man with a disability) and privilege (e.g., White and male). Assignments can be viewed as being about both aspects, making for more nuanced discussion about the relative strengths, salience, and impacts of both disadvantage and privilege.

What If You Have Never Taught About Disability? My assumption is that readers will range from instructors who have not taught about disability before or only minimally, to those who regularly teach about disability but may want more options to try. If you feel trepidation about giving assignments, remember that each activity comes with explicit directions, any necessary handouts, possible grading rubrics, and talking points. The assignments in Part B are simpler in several respects. They require less instructor or student preparation. The concepts covered are less complex and nuanced than those in Part C. No special student skills are required, such as interviewing skills. Grading is often bimodal: The student either did or did not do the assignment.

What If You Yourself Hold Biases and Stereotypes About People with Disabilities? One problem that can arise when people talk about disability is that they get tongue-tied trying to use "correct" language and avoid displaying their own ignorance and/or preconceptions. It can be helpful if the instructor talks first about gaps in knowledge, beliefs learned in childhood, or current questions about disability, as a way to open up the class to free discussion. Of course you hold biases and stereotypes—we all do! You are not modeling perfection for students but a willingness to engage with material, honestly reevaluate your own preconceived notions, and examine where those notions came from.

What If You Have a Visible or Hidden Disability? For myself (a person with a visible disability), sometimes my obvious disability inhibits an audience out of fear that they will insult me (or so I presume). One way around this is to have students write questions on a 3 × 5 card and collect the cards before I see them so that I do not know who asked which question. I find that I get more open inquiries this way. In addition, being able to ask me personal questions allows them access they likely would not otherwise have. But it is important to remember that when you know one person with a disability, *you know one person with a disability*. If your disability is hidden, you are under no obligation to disclose it unless you feel comfortable doing so and believe it would be educational.

Do I Need to Read the Research Base in Chapter 2**?** Although I obviously prefer that you do because it informs the exercises in this book, it is not necessary to understand the exercises. I do believe the research base would be helpful in debriefing the exercises, however. But there is one caveat—In Chapter 2 I discuss the evidence *against* using disability simulations to address attitudes about or behaviors toward persons with disabilities. *So please do not use simulations without reading at least that portion of* Chapter 2.

General Instructions: It can be tempting to simply state the directions, give the handouts, and let students do the activities. However, as with most homework, clear guidance increases the value. Thus, for each activity I suggest the following guidelines: (a) state the objectives clearly; (b) be sure everyone has the same understanding of the activity; (c) engage in any recommended pre-discussion stated with the activity; (d) acknowledge and work through hesitation or reluctance on the part of participants prior to doing the activity; (e) debrief thoroughly, allowing for both positive and negative outcomes; and (f) illustrate challenges and solutions related to both the individual and the systemic levels.

References

American Psychological Association. (2010). *Publication manual of the American Psychological Association* (6th ed.). Washington, DC: Author.

American Psychological Association. (2020). *Publication manual of the American Psychological Association* (7th ed.). Washington, DC: Author.

2 Attitudes, Knowledge, and Behavior

WHAT WE ALREADY KNOW

WHAT ARE THE goals of the activities in this book? What impact might they have, and how will that impact help the population of persons with disabilities? Generally, courses and workshops on diversity target attitudes, knowledge, and behavior, often in that order. Frequently, the desired goal is to change people's behaviors. Examples include getting people to perform good oral hygiene, recycle garbage, reduce water consumption, buy organic produce, take public transportation—these are examples of behaviors that bestow individual or public good. But public good is not always a sufficient motivator. For example, water consumption during drought is higher in high-income areas where the increased cost is not a deterrent. Effecting behavioral change may require different methods for different populations. In the case of disability, knowledge and awareness are not sufficient if they are not accompanied by behavioral changes. And for trainees, increased skills in working with clients with disabilities is a key outcome.

It is often assumed that changing people's attitudes toward disability will have several positive effects: (a) increasing contact with people with disabilities; (b) reducing anxiety and discomfort when interacting with people with disabilities; (c) reducing stereotyping and prejudice and thus discrimination; and (d) becoming allies and advocates for disability issues. Unfortunately, we cannot say that any of these will be the result. Becoming an ally and advocate may take more than a change in attitude; it may require a more profound change in worldview about ability differences.

Teaching Disability. Rhoda Olkin, Oxford University Press. © Oxford University Press 2021.
DOI: 10.1093/oso/9780190850661.003.0002

Do attitudes change behaviors, vice versa, or bidirectionally? It is important that we understand the direction of causation between attitudes and behaviors, and this understanding can become the basis for policies and programs designed to effect behavioral change (Kroesen, Handy, & Chorus, 2017). If attitudes and behavior are misaligned, it is possible that behavior will affect attitudes to be more aligned than that attitudes will affect behavior (Kroesen et al., 2017).

The Basis for Attitudes Toward Disability

Prejudice is an antipathy toward a group and the members of that stigmatized group (Allport, 1954). Stigma can stem from three types of grouping (Goffman, 1963): tribal identities; "abominations of the body" (p. 14; e.g., some types of disabilities); and blemishes of individual character (e.g., mental illness and some types of cognitive disabilities). The last two groups elicit strong negative emotional reactions of fear, disgust, or aversion.

Social categorization puts people into groups based on an attribute (e.g., disability). Differences within a group are minimized and differences across groups are maximized. Furthermore, those differences are often presumed to be inherent to the group, generalized to other attributes, and applied to individuals within the group (Dovidio, Pagatto, & Hebl, 2011). The stereotype content model posits that perceptions of groups are based on the dimensions of warmth and competence (Cuddy, Fiske, & Glick, 2007; Fiske, Cuddy, Glick & Xu, 2002). Groups perceived as high in warmth but low in competence—such as people with disabilities—elicit pity and sympathy.

Disability encompasses a wide variety of conditions, but specific features of a given disability will engender different degrees of stigma. These conditions include visibility or concealability; aesthetic qualities; actual or perceived origin or cause; probable course of the condition and its degree of uncertainty and uncontrollability; disruptiveness or interference to interpersonal communication; and degree of perceived peril to others (Livneh, Chan, & Kaya, 2014).

A comprehensive examination of attitudes toward disability (Yuker, 1988) indicated that, on the whole, attitudes toward disability "are complex and multifaceted" (p. xii) and not easily understood or changed. Nonetheless, Yuker argued that we must understand, measure, and change attitudes if we want to improve the status of people with disabilities. He made eight recommendations: (a) cease using univariate approaches to studying attitudes toward disability; (b) examine both negative and positive attitudes; (c) investigate sources of attitudes, including culture, experiences, teachings, and intrapsychic variables; (d) develop better measures of attitudes;

(e) pay special attention to professionals and peers who interact with persons with disabilities; (f) evaluate both short- and long-term changes effected by multidimensional programs designed to change attitudes; (g) study the complex relations between attitudes and behavior; and (h) put disability into the context of the entire person, of which disability is only one part.

An understanding of the social psychology of disability illuminates interactions with disabled people (Dunn, 2015, 2016). Outsiders view disability as a defining quality, that is, they *essentialize* the disability. This leads to the *fundamental negative bias*, a focus on the perceived negative quality of the other. Generally, bad outweighs good, so perceived negative qualities diminish the impact of positive qualities. This forms the basis for the mostly negative attitudes toward disability. Disability is highly stigmatized and marks those with a disability as "other," such that they are treated as fundamentally different from those without disabilities. This difference then promotes devaluation, prejudice, and negative stereotypes, leading to discrimination.

Wright (1988) discussed the fundamental negative bias as a product of saliency, value, and context. If something observed stands out (saliency), and that which is observed is regarded as negative (value), and its context is vague (context), then "the negative value assigned to the object of observation will be a major factor in guiding perception, thinking, and feeling to fit its negative character" (p. 5). Thus, it would seem important that activities designed to affect attitudes put disability into a context, rather than focusing on disability as an abstract or single variable. "The problems associated with disability are not usually personal or dispositional but are generally external and situational (e.g., environmental constraints, such as the absence of Braille signage or accommodating ramps or elevators; social constraints, ranging from well-meaning, but sometimes imprudent, comments made by bystanders, to inappropriate curiosity and prejudicial attitudes)" (p. 114).

Although attitudes toward persons with disabilities are generally negative, there is conversely strong support for the notions of fairness and equity on a societal level. For example, companies that hire people with disabilities are viewed more favorably than companies that don't, and people state they are more inclined to do business with such companies (Dovidio et al., 2011). A review of employers' attitudes toward the Americans with Disabilities Act indicated that most employers favored the act but had reservations about specific accommodations. Furthermore, there is a gap between expressed willingness to hire employees with disabilities and actual hiring practices (Araten-Bergman, 2016; Hernandez, Keys, & Balcazar, 2000). Despite support for the notion of equity, wages for employees with disabilities are lower than those for nondisabled employees (Johnson & Baldwin, 1993). A perspective on this ambivalence (Dovidio et al, 2011) suggests that psychological tension is created that will be resolved by amplifying in one direction or the other. If a person believes in fair treatment of people with disabilities but is unable to enact that fairness, the tension might be ameliorated by blaming the disabled person or viewing them as individually unworthy. It may be that the conflict is created by dissonance between explicit and implicit bias (see following section). For example, the explicit attitude is that those with disabilities should be treated fairly, and the implicit bias is more negative toward persons with disabilities.

Implicit and Explicit Bias

Between the time of Yuker's (1988) and Nario-Redmond's (2020) books, studies on implicit bias were published—over five million studies in at least 20 countries and 16 languages (Nosek et al., 2007). These studies measured reaction time to stimuli, with the assumption that reaction times are faster for stimuli that are closely related in memory than those more distantly related. For example, it would take less time to link a negative word (e.g., unfortunate) than a positive word (e.g., robust) to disability if the person considers disability a negative category. Speed is then used to infer the strength of association between terms. (For a critique of Implicit Attitude Test methodology and assumptions, see Brownstein, Madva, & Gawronski, 2020). Many studies have yielded results showing negative associations to disability, even among those who work with people with disabilities (Antonak & Livneh, 2000; Brodwin & Orange, 2002; Guglielmi, 1999; Reeve, 2000; Robey, Beckley, & Kirschner, 2006; Wilson & Scior, 2014). Furthermore, there is little or even negative correlation between implicit and explicit (i.e., conscious) bias (Dovidio et al., 2011).

A study in the United States of changes to explicit and implicit bias between 2007 and 2016 indicated changes in explicit bias from negative toward neutrality for six groups: sexual orientation, race, skin tone, age, disability, and body weight (Charlesworth & Banaji, 2019). Similarly, implicit bias moved toward neutrality for sexual orientation, race, and skin tone. However, implicit bias toward disability was stable over that time. The weakest correlations between explicit and implicit bias were found for disability and age attitudes. There was no prediction in either direction between explicit and implicit attitudes toward disability, implying that these are affected by different processes. Changes in population-level implicit attitudes for three conditions (race, skin tone, sexuality) suggest that "implicit attitudes can be gradually and durably changed at the population level, in the direction of decreasing prejudice" (p. 189). The question remains concerning why this was not evidenced for disability (or weight and age).

At the individual level, implicit attitudes can be altered, and at least two studies showed short-term changes to implicit attitudes (Dasgupta, 2013; Lai et al., 2014).

However, attempts to change long-term implicit attitudes have been unsuccessful or unduplicated (Charlesworth & Banaji, 2019). Generally, lower implicit bias is found for females, liberals, younger persons, persons of color, and those less educated (Nosek et al., 2007). Changing implicit bias may be important as implicit attitude change preceded explicit change for race and skin tone (Charlesworth & Banaji, 2019). However, it may be that the mechanisms of change are different for disability. We have to assume for now that changing both explicit and implicit bias toward disability involves separate endeavors, but that both must be addressed if we are to make population-level changes to reduce discrimination against people with disabilities.

Implicit and explicit bias will differentially influence behavior. Explicit bias will be activated in conditions that are well thought out, deliberate, and take more time. Implicit bias affects more rapid or spontaneous responses and nonverbal behaviors (Dovidio et al., 2011). Nonverbal behaviors have included reduced gesturing, increased interpersonal distance, behavioral inhibition, avoidance, and signs of anxiety (e.g., averted gaze, blinking, closed posture). These manifestations of implicit bias can be apparent in therapy when a clinician holds overtly positive attitudes but negative implicit bias displayed in nonverbal ways. These might include delay in shaking hands, pausing before using a word related to disability, staring while trying not to stare, averting eye contact, or minimizing spontaneous movements. These cues will be apparent to clients with disabilities who have lots of experience with the reactions of others. Ultimately, changes to implicit bias are necessary for therapy to be disability affirmative and culturally appropriate.

Changing Attitudes Toward Disability

An excellent review of almost three decades worth of efforts to diminish prejudice toward people with disabilities concluded that most studies focused on attitudes and bias (Nario-Redmond, 2020). Very few studies have targeted behaviors, activism, or disability rights. Nario-Redmond noted that the measured outcomes of most studies are liking, reduced discomfort, and less stigmatizing attitudes. It is questionable whether these outcomes would lead to behavioral changes toward people with disabilities. Nonetheless, for the purpose of affecting how clinicians interact with clients with disabilities, reduced discomfort and stigmatization are important and necessary—but not sufficient—steps toward equitable treatment. Activities that target these steps can be a beginning toward more culturally informed (and presumably effective) therapy.

A review and meta-analysis of 12 studies designed to affect children's attitudes toward people with disabilities was conducted (Armstrong, Morris, Abraham, &

Tarrant, 2017). The selected studies were conducted in schools and based on the contact hypothesis, namely, that increased contact with people with disabilities—whether in real life, imagery, in the media—will improve attitudes toward disability. "The 'contact hypothesis' describes the positive impact that direct face-to-face interactions can have on people's attitudes towards members of different social groups" (p. 11):

Results indicated that direct contact improved attitudes, but media contact did not. This is disappointing in that media campaigns can reach a large number of children. However, there were only two studies using media contact, and they produced opposite results. Furthermore, the authors noted that "despite the promising findings from these contact interventions, the quality and the reporting within most studies was judged to be relatively poor for a variety of reasons including lack of baseline data, failure to report effect sizes, and failure to conduct a priori sample size calculations" (Armstrong et al., 2017, p. 21). Although none of the studies used simulation, the authors nonetheless discussed simulation tasks (which I discuss further in this chapter).

In one of the few published activities designed to illustrate how people think about disabilities, Wright (1988) described an exercise she called the "mine-thine problem" that highlights the differences in perspectives of insiders and outsiders. Participants are asked to write down the initials of five people they know well, and for each person they are to indicate that person's worst handicap, disadvantage, limitation, shortcoming, or problem. Then next to each person, they are to write their own worst handicap. For each pair, participants circle the one they would choose for themselves if it were possible to choose. Group results indicated that participants would select their own handicap at least 60% of the time, usually more, even if their own handicap is objectively more impairing. Wright explained that participants are used to their own handicap (familiarity) and have learned ways to deal with it (coping), and it is part of the self (self-identity). Participants are insiders to their own handicap and familiar with its context, versus outsiders to the others' handicaps, which are less contextualized.

Why Not to Use Simulation Exercises

Simulation exercises attempt to create a situation as close to the real one as possible to give participants an experience they could not otherwise have or to allow practice in a safe context. Examples might be giving injections into an orange, using a flight simulator, or practicing cardiopulmonary resuscitation on a dummy (Burgstahler & Doe, 2004). None of the activities in this book are simulation exercises.

Although widely used on college campuses and often very popular, there are several good reasons these are not advisable means of exploring disability. First, they do not in fact simulate disability, as living with and acclimating to a disability is not the same as acting disabled for a few hours or even a day (Dunn, 2016). For example, a novice using a wheelchair for 1 day discounts the experience and skills more permanent users would possess. Second, it puts the focus on the physical aspects and difficulties related to disability, although the psychosocial, interpersonal, and systemic issues are more paramount for people with disabilities (Dunn, Fisher, & Beard, 2012). Third, it implies that only through direct experience can one learn about disability and downplays the lived experiences and stories of people with disabilities themselves. "Mental health knowledge is dominated by professional knowledge to the exclusion of the knowledge based on lived experience (experiential knowledge) that people with mental health problems can bring" (Faulkner, 2017, p. 500). Fourth, it is insulting to have able-bodied people imitate disabilities, akin to a White person putting on blackface. Do we really believe that one can never gain understanding of the "other" without mimicking the other? Fifth, those conducting simulation studies usually measure intended outcomes (e.g., empathy) but not unintended consequences (e.g., increased pity) and only in the immediate aftermath of the simulation. Initial measures tend to capture enthusiasm and emotional engagement in the simulation. However, more distal measures can show more negative attitudes, as simulation focuses on what people with disabilities cannot do. This emphasis is on the intrapersonal limitations rather than the design of the environment or the adaptations people make to disability over time. (For two critiques of simulations, see French, 1992, and Scullion, 1996.)

The Activities in This Book

Some activities in this book target increased awareness—not about disability itself but about the barriers, disadvantages, hidden costs, microaggressions, and discrimination faced by people with disabilities. The underlying theory is the social model of disability (Olkin, 1999, 2017), wherein disability primarily results from the disadvantages imposed by society. Because there is so often a mismatch between the needs of a person with a disability and the built, social, and system environment, a heavy burden is placed on disabled persons to fight for, derive, and finagle their own accommodations. Many activities focus on these burdens. The target actors for the activities are people who, in their professional roles, will be working with clients with disabilities. My hope is that these activities will be enlightening about the systemic, political, and personal challenges confronted by their clients with disabilities, changing both explicit and implicit attitudes, and that these changes will prompt clinicians to become committed activists and allies. However, that outcome is not guaranteed. It is entirely possible that there are unintended consequences, such as increases in pity, or reinforcing beliefs that disabled people are superhumans, courageous, or inspirational. Therefore, I strongly encourage instructors to assess outcomes. Toward that end, I have included a chapter on possible outcome measures. I invite you to submit your experiences with the activities and any outcome data to http://www.rolkin.com.

References

Allport, G. W. (1954). *The nature of prejudice.* Cambridge, MA: Addison-Wesley.

Antonak, R. F., & Livneh, H. (2000). Measurement of attitudes towards persons with disabilities. *Disabilities and Rehabilitation, 22*, 211–224.

Araten-Bergman, T. (2016). Managers' hiring intentions and the actual hiring of qualified workers with disabilities. *International Journal of Human Resource Management, 27*(14), 1510–1530. https://doi.org/10.1080/09585192.2015.1128466

Armstrong, M., Morris, C., Abraham, C., & Tarrant, M. (2017). Interventions utilising contact with people with disabilities to improve children's attitudes towards disability: A systematic review and meta-analysis. *Disability and Health Journal, 10*, 11–22.

Brodwin, M. G., & Orange, L. M. (2002). Attitudes toward disability. In J. D. Andrew & C. W. Faubion (Eds.), *Rehabilitation services: An introduction for the human service professionals* (pp. 174–197). Osage Beach, MO: Aspen Professional Services.

Brownstein, M., Madva, A., & Gawronski, B. (2020). Understanding implicit bias: Putting the criticism into perspective. *Pacific Philosophical Quarterly, 101*(2), 276–307. https://doi.org/10.1111/papq.12302

Burgstahler, S., & Doe, T. (2004). Disability-related simulations: If, when, and how to use them in professional development. *Review of Disability Studies, 1*(2), 8–18.

Charlesworth, T. E. S., & Banaji, M. R. (2019). Patterns of implicit and explicit attitudes: I. Long-term change and stability over 2007 to 2016. *Psychological Science, 30*(2), 174–192. https://doi.org/10.1177/0956797618813087

Cuddy, A. J. C., Fiske, S. T., & Glick, P. (2007). The BIAS map: Behaviors from intergroup affect and stereotypes. *Journal of Personality and Social Psychology, 92*, 631–648.

Dasgupta, N. (2013). Implicit attitudes and beliefs adapt to situations: A decade of research on the malleability of implicit prejudice, stereotypes, and the self-concept. In P. Devine & A. Plant (Eds.), *Advances in experimental social psychology* (Vol. 47, pp. 233–279). San Diego, CA: Academic Press. https://doi.org/10.1016/B978-0-12-407236-7.00005-X

Dovidio, J. F., Pagatto, L., & Hebl, M. R. (2011). Implicit attitudes and discrimination against people with physical disabilities. In R. L. Weiner & S. L. Wilborn (Eds.), *Disability and age discrimination: Perspectives in law and psychology* (pp. 157–184). New York: Springer. https://doi./10.1007/978-1-4419-6293-5_9

Dunn, D. S. (2015). *The social psychology of disability*. New York: Oxford University Press.

Dunn, D. S. (2016). Teaching about psychosocial aspects of disability: Emphasizing person-environment relations. *Teaching of Psychology*, 1–8. doi:10.1177009862831664949 2.

Dunn, D. S., Fisher, D. J., & Beard, B. M. (2012). Revisiting the mine/thine problem: A sensitizing exercise for clinic, classroom, and attributional research. *Rehabilitation Psychology, 57*(2), 113–123.

Faulkner, A. (2017). Survivor research and Mad Studies: The role and value of experiential knowledge in mental health research. *Disability & Society, 32*(4), 500–520.

Fiske, S. T., Cuddy, A. J. C., Glick, P., & Xu, J. (2002). A model of (often mixed) stereotype content: Competence and warmth respectively follow from perceived status and competence. *Journal of Personality and Social Psychology, 44*, 600–607.

French, S. (1992). Simulation exercises in disability awareness training: A critique. *Disability, Handicap and Society, 7*, 257–266.

Goffman, I. (1963). *Stigma: Notes on the management of a spoiled identity.* Englewood Cliffs, NJ: Prentice-Hall.

Guglielmi, R. S. (1999). Psychophysiological assessment of prejudice: Past research, current status, and future directions. *Personality and Social Psychology Review, 3*, 123–157.

Hernandez, B., Keys, C., & Balcazar, F. (2000). Employer attitudes toward workers with disabilities and their ADA employment rights: A literature review. *Journal of Rehabilitation, 66*(4), 4–16.

Johnson, W. G., & Baldwin, M. (1993). The American with Disabilities Act: Will it make a difference? *Policy Studies Journal, 21*(4), 775–788. https://doi.org/10.1111/j.1541-0072.1993.tb02174.x

Kroesen, M., Handy, S., & Chorus, C., (2017). Do attitudes cause behavior or vice versa? An alternative conceptualization of the attitude-behavior relationship in travel behavior modeling. *Transportation Research Part A: Policy and Practice, 101*, 190–202. https://doi.org/10.1016/j.tra.2017.05.013

Lai, C. K., Marini, M., Lehr, S. A., Cerruti, C., Shin, J. E. L., Joy-Gaba, J. A., . . . Nosek, B. A. (2014). Reducing implicit racial preferences: I. A comparative investigation of 17 interventions. *Journal of Experimental Psychology: General, 143*, 1765–1785. https://doi:10.1037/a0036260

Livneh, H., Chan, F., & Kaya, C. (2014). Stigma related to physical and sensory disabilities. In P. W. Corrigan (Ed.), *The stigma of disease and disability: Understanding causes and overcoming injustices* (pp. 93–120). Washington, DC: American Psychological Association. https://doi.org/10.1037/14297-006

Nario-Redmond, M. R. (2020). *Ableism: The causes and consequences of disability prejudice.* Hoboken, NJ: Wiley.

Nosek, B. A., Smyth, F. L., Hansen, J. J., Devos, T., Lindner, N. M., Ranganath, K. A., . . . Banaji, M. R. (2007). Pervasiveness and correlates of implicit attitudes and stereotypes. *European Review of Social Psychology, 18*, 36–88. https://doi.org/10.1080/10463280701489053

Olkin, R. (1999). *What psychotherapists should know about disability.* New York: Guilford Press.

Olkin, R. (2017). *Disability-affirmative therapy: A template for understanding your clients with disabilities.* New York: Oxford University Press.

Reeve, D. (2000). Oppression within the counseling room. *Disability and Society, 15*, 669–682.

Robey, K. L., Beckley, L., & Kirschner, M. (2006). Implicit infantilizing attitudes about disability. *Journal of Developmental and Physical Disabilities, 18*, 441–453.

Scullion, P. (1996). Quasidisability experiences using simulation. *British Journal of Therapy and Rehabilitation, 4*, 292–293.

Wilson, M. C., & Scior, K. (2014). Attitudes towards individuals with disabilities as measured by the Implicit Association Test: A literature review.

Wright, B. A. (1988). Attitudes and the fundamental negative bias: Conditions and corrections. In H. E. Yuker (Ed.), *Attitudes toward persons with disabilities* (pp. 3–21). New York: Springer.

Yuker, H. E. (Ed.). (1988). *Attitudes toward persons with disabilities.* New York: Springer.

B Beginning-Level Exercises

APPROACHING A NEW area of diversity usually starts with basic knowledge about the group in question. But, that exploration may be more meaningful if students can make discoveries on their own rather than being "spoon-fed." The activities in this chapter guide those discoveries. By combining activities done individually (e.g., computer searches) and discussion in class, students learn on their own as well as from each other. Debriefing from the instructor is important, as there is always the possibility of unintended consequences. For example, a student researching a specific diagnosis they have been assigned may feel increased pity or anxiety about the possibility of disability.

The first assignment relates to the language used to describe disabilities in various venues (e.g., news, traffic reports, clinical settings). Another assignment has students explore the links between economics and disability—how they are reciprocally related. Assignments also focus on employment rates and whether/how they have been affected by nondiscrimination laws. Intersectionality is explored by having students use their own demographic status (gender, ethnicity, sexual orientation, religion, national origin) and researching the intersectionality of two (or more) identities in both professional and lay literature. (Two more activities on intersectionality are in Chapter 9.)

One method of learning about different cultures involves hearing from persons within those cultures. There are several documentaries about and by people with disabilities that offer effective insider viewpoints (*Crip Camp*; *Best Boy; Gleason; King Gimp; Sexability; When Billy Broke His Head*). There also are blogs, podcasts, and autobiographies. Readers do not need to be limited by the ones suggested in the following activities. In Chapter 8, I list films and YouTube videos that students have found interesting and informative.

3 Exploring the Basics

Activity 3.1: Exploration of Language

Activity: Students should go online to the World Health Organization website and read the definitions of handicap, impairment, and disability (see Handout 3.1). The Additional Reading at the end of this activity could be assigned as well.

Where: Reading portion can be done in class or as homework, but discussion should be in class.

Purpose: To explore the use of language and how it both leads (anticipates?) and follows important social and conceptual changes.

Learning Objectives

1. To differentiate terms used to describe illness and disability.
2. To explore how language reflects social changes.
3. To understand how word usage introduces new concepts to the general population.

Materials: Internet access.

Preparation: None.

Time: 30–60 minutes, depending on size of class and degree of participation.

Teaching Disability. Rhoda Olkin, Oxford University Press. © Oxford University Press 2021.
DOI: 10.1093/oso/9780190850661.003.0003

Possible Outcomes: Positive outcomes could be better understanding of the relations between language and social construction and of important distinctions related to chronic illness, health conditions, handicap, impairment, and disability. Negative outcomes might be some anxiety as value-laden words are used, and students might be shy about using certain words, not knowing if they are politically correct.

Talking Points: Have this list of words available for students during this discussion: *Colored, Negro, Black, African American; girls, ladies, women, female, gender; illegal immigrant, undocumented residents; heterosexual, homosexual, gay, lesbian, bisexual, transgender, transsexual, gender queer, nonbinary.* Note how the changes in what words are commonly used are accompanied by changes in society. Have students associate different words with the era in which they were used and the broad social events of those times. (You could use the television series *Mad Men* as an example of how women were referred to in the 1950s and the implications in the workplace.) If a student (or instructor) has a disability, have them define their own impairment, handicap, and disability to show the distinctions. For example, my *impairment* is polio (note how little this tells you about functioning), my *handicap* is mobility limitations and fatigue, my *disability* is environmental barriers such as stairs, changes to social interactions such as people patting me on the head, and economic disadvantage.

Grading Rubric: Should not be graded, or it could stifle open discussion. Could be part of points for "participation."

Handouts: 3.1: Instructions for Students.

Additional Reading

Kostanisek, N. (2011). Use of the International Classification of Functioning, Disability, and Health (ICF) as a conceptual framework and common language for disability statistics and health information systems. *BMC Public Health*, *11*(Suppl. 4), S3. https://doi.org/10.1186/1471-2458-11-S4-S3

Handout 3.1: Instructions for Students

This assignment has two parts: (A) You are to go online to find the definitions of three words: *handicap, impairment*, and *disability*, according to the World Health Organization (https://www.who.int) and bring these definitions to class. Also find definitions for *chronic illness* and *health conditions*. (Optional: find a current article that uses those terms.) (B) Now consider these three words in the context of the definition of disability used in the Rehabilitation Act (1973) and the Americans with Disabilities Act (1990):

A person with a disability is someone who (a) has a physical or mental impairment that substantially limits one or more "major life activities," (b) has a record of such an impairment, or (c) is regarded as having such an impairment.

Important note: Do not use Wikipedia as the source for your definitions.

Activity 3.2: Exploring Your New Diagnosis

Activity: Each student investigates his or her assigned chronic health condition (CHC)/disability.

Where: At home, online.

Purpose: To mirror the experience a person might have when finding out they have a CHC or disability and to differentiate more and less reliable sources of information.

Learning objectives

1. To experience investigating a new diagnosis online.
2. To locate reliable (and unreliable) sources of information.
3. To self-examine emotional reactions in reading about an assigned diagnosis.

Materials: Handout 3.2a: Instructions for Instructor with a list of possible diagnoses to assign to students. The assigned diagnoses may be kept for other assignments and would be needed for assignments further in this book. No student should be assigned a diagnosis that he or she, or his or her child, actually has. Handout 3.2b: Instructions for Students, with instructions for the assignment.

Preparation: None.

Time: Request that students spend 2 hours on this assignment.

Possible Outcomes: Students usually start by just typing in the name of their diagnosis into Google. This gives an overwhelming list of possible sites. Generally, the first step is to find out the basic information about the symptoms and process of diagnosis for this CHC. So "overwhelmed" is often the first thing students report. Second, once they hear someone talk about living with the CHC or disability, they notice whether it is a visible or hidden disability and hear what the main symptoms are that interfere with activities of daily living. All of this can lead to a negative view of what it means to have this CHC, which makes the talking points important. You don't want to leave students with this view only.

Talking Points: Discussion will usually first focus on the emotional responses to doing this assignment, and little guidance is needed. But then it can be important to counter some of the bleak view that might emerge. It is helpful to be ready to show a TED Talk from someone living with a CHC or disability who paints a more positive picture. Then you might revisit the language used to describe a CHC and disability; what view of the CHC or disability do the words suggest? Another important talking point relates to intersectionality: As students were researching their assigned CHC or disability, did they find materials and information that seemed to apply to themselves (i.e., mirrored their own gender, age, ethnicity, sexual orientation)? Did they find information about disparities in prevalence across different groups? Was there something they found that felt inclusive or exclusive of their identity?

Grading Rubric: A point system is suggested on Handout 3.2a: Instructions for Teachers for a total of 15 points broken down by task. Alternatively, this can be an all-or-nothing assignment, either full points awarded for doing the assignment and posting it online or distributing it in class, and no points for not doing the assignment.

Handouts: 3.2a: Instructions for Teachers; 3.2b: Instructions for Students.

Additional Reading

Burcaw, S. (2017). *Not so different: What you really want to ask about having a disability.* New York: Roaring Press Books.

Montez, J. K., Hayward, M. D., & Wolf, D. A. (2017). Do U.S. states' socioeconomic and policy contexts shape differences in adult disability? *Social Science & Medicine, 178*, 115–126.

Thomas, P. (2005). *Don't call me special: A first look at disability.* Hauppage, NH: Barron's educational series.

Handout 3.2a: Instructions for Teachers

Each student is "assigned" a CHC or disability. They are to spend a minimum of 2 hours researching this CHC or disability online, according to the directions on Handout 3.2b: Instructions for Students.

To Assign Chronic Conditions or Disabilities: Put each diagnosis from the table below on a separate piece of paper and have students pick one. It is acceptable if they trade among themselves. If a student happens to select his or her own disorder, have available more diagnoses that have not been assigned so the student can make a trade privately with you without having to disclose to the class (in cases of invisible disabilities); remember to announce this possibility to the class before distributing the disabilities.

List of Potential Diagnoses:

Ankylosing spondylitis Attention deficit hyperactivity disorder, combined type Asthma Autism Blindness Bipolar disorder Cerebral palsy (since this occurs from birth, the person is to imagine that they have never been told much about the disability other than that they "walk funny") Chronic obstructive pulmonary disease Chronic kidney disease Congenital heart disease (specifically coarctation of the aorta, newly discovered) Crohn's disease Diabetes, insulin dependent Epilepsy	Fibromyalgia Little person (dwarfism) Lupus (systemic lupus erythematosus lupus) Multiple sclerosis, relapsing and remitting Multiple sclerosis, primary progressive Osteoarthritis Scleroderma Sickle cell disease Spinal cord injury (T3 level) Spinal cord injury (C6 level) Tourette syndrome combined with obsessive–compulsive disorder Traumatic brain injury (from explosion, but no brain penetration) Turner syndrome Williams syndrome

This is what students will be asked to do, and a suggested number of points per item:

1. Find a reliable source (Do you suggest some, like WebMD or the Mayo Clinic site?) of basic information about this condition. Information to be included (but not necessarily limited to)

a. What is the nature of your disability (e.g., what is it, when and how did you get it, is it life threatening, does it get better/worse/stay the same?)? (2 points)
b. How does the disability vary for different people (e.g., gender, age, ethnicity, country)? (2 points)
c. Describe the effects of your disability on functioning (e.g., communication, mobility, cognition, vision, learning, working, and driving). (2 points)
d. What are the likely psychosocial effects of your disability? (2 points)
e. How does your own culture (religion, sexual orientation, ethnicity) respond to your disability? (2 points)
f. Does your disability make you more likely to experience depression, anxiety, or post-traumatic stress disorder (PTSD)? (2 points)

2. (b) Find a YouTube video of someone living with your assigned condition. (1 point)
3. (c) Find a TED Talk about your assigned (or a very similar) condition. (1 point)
4. (d) Find the national organization devoted to this CHC or disability. (1 point)

Total: 15 points

Handout 3.2b: Instructions for Students

You have been "assigned" a CHC or disability. Please spend a minimum of 2 hours researching this CHC or disability online:

1. Find a reliable source of basic information about this condition. Information to be included (but not necessarily limited to)
   a. What is the nature of your disability? (e.g., what is it, when and how did you get it, is it life threatening, does it get better/worse/stay the same?).
   b. How does the disability vary for different people (e.g., gender, age, ethnicity, country)?
   c. Describe the effects of your disability on functioning (e.g., communication, mobility, cognition, vision, learning, working, and driving.).
   d. What are the likely psychosocial effects of your disability?
   e. How does your own culture (religion, sexual orientation, ethnicity) respond to your disability?
   f. Does your disability make you more likely to experience depression, anxiety, or PTSD?
2. Find a YouTube of someone living with your assigned condition.
3. Find a TED Talk about your assigned (or a very similar) condition.
4. Find the national organization devoted to this CHC or disability.

Activity 3.3: Movies Versus Real Life

Activity: Compare the depiction of a real person with a disability in film with the biography of that same person.

Where: Watching the movie can be done either in class or at home. Researching the biography of the person depicted will be online.

Purpose: Outsider and insider views of disability are very different, and this basic fact is very important to the understanding of CHC or disability. Students will compare the two views.

Learning Objectives

1. To compare and contrast a media depiction of a real person with a disability versus the person's biography or autobiography.
2. To explore what gets highlighted and what gets left out in media depictions.
3. To learn the value of firsthand reports.

Materials: Film, handout.

Preparation: None.

Time: Approximately 1 hour 45 minutes to view the film *My Left Foot,* about 1 hour to read biographical or autobiographic materials online, and 1 hour to write out answers to questions on the handout. *Note to instructors*: (a) This can be used as a class discussion or a written assignment. However, if done in as a class discussion, have students write out their responses to these questions at home and come prepared to discuss them. (b) In Chapter 4, there is an assignment related to *King Gimp,* a documentary about a man with cerebral palsy. It can be interesting to contrast *My Left Foot* with *King Gimp* (which is Activity 4.1).

Possible Outcomes: The film is very powerful and well acted, so students are likely to have many emotional reactions to it. This is why the assignment has them write out answers to questions at home, so they have a bit of processing time.

Talking Points: Christy Brown's parents were encouraged to institutionalize him; consider the economic and social forces that encouraged this action and those that mitigated against it. A key point in the film (and in Christy's life) concerns his mother and the steadfast role she played in encouraging her son. This is a common theme in disability success stories—a parent (usually the mother) who takes on incredible advocacy and encouragement roles, often against medical or professional advice. (This theme emerges again in the documentary *King Gimp*, which has an assignment in Chapter 4.) In the case of the Brown family, the mother took on these roles despite having 22 children, 9 of whom died in infancy, and not being wealthy. His mother has been referred to as "a saint"; this idea of only the saintly doing this for a son would be an excellent point for discussion. Additionally, the real-life Christy Brown, married to Mary Carr, died from choking, possibly being neglected, and was found with bruises on his body. His first romantic relationship with Beth Moore included her withholding alcohol until he wrote the requisite number of pages each day—is this abuse? Consider discussing the higher incidence of abuse (sexual, physical, financial) of people with disabilities.

Grading Rubric: If done as a written assignment, 2 points per question, based on writing (1 point) and quality of introspection (1 point). If done as discussion, all points awarded if student did the written portion as requested and participated in discussion.

Handout: 3.3: Instructions for Students.

Additional Reading

Hays, M. T., & Black, R. S. (2003). Troubling signs: Disability, Hollywood movies and the construction of a discourse of pity. *Disability Studies Quarterly, 23*(2), 114–132.

Handout 3.3: Instructions for Students

This homework has three parts:

Part A: Watch the film *My Left Foot.*

Part B: Then address the following questions about the film:

1. Could a person with cerebral palsy have played the role? Why do you think an able-bodied actor was chosen to play this role? What does this imply about the perspective of the director? How do you see the director's perspective in the film?
2. What were your initial reactions to Christy's impairments? How did those change over time as the film went on?
3. What was the response of the mother toward Christy? How did she make a difference in his life?
4. What role did socioeconomic status play in Christy's childhood?
5. How were romance and sexuality handled in the film?
6. What prevented Christy from getting a formal education? What accommodations would have been necessary for him to attend school?
7. Christy was a White Irish male; consider what might have been different if he had been gay or he had been a female.
8. How did the film differ from Christy Brown's real life?

Part C: Go online and read as much as you can in the space of about 1 hour about the real life of Christy Brown. Note overlaps and discrepancies between the film and Brown's biography.

Activity 3.4: News Media Depictions

Activity: Find a news story about a person with a disability from the past 6 months in the newspaper, online, or in *Time* or *Newsweek.*

Where: At home or online, with in-class discussion.

Purpose: To explore how attitudes are shaped by news media and how news media reflect societal attitudes.

Learning Objectives

1. To see how people with disabilities are depicted in the news.
2. To reflect on the language and attitudes inherent in the depiction.
3. To conceptualize the social framework of disability.

Materials: Handout with instructions; access to newspapers, Internet, or *Time* or *Newsweek* magazine. Optional: Have each student give to classmates a copy of the story they found so that the entire collection can be examined.

Preparation: It is helpful if the instructor has a recent example to discuss before students do the assignment. Newspaper stories about disability often appear in the "lifestyle" section of newspapers. Sometimes people with disabilities are mentioned in an ancillary way in a story ostensibly about something else (e.g., California's 2017 law on right to die might mention protesters with disabilities in one or two lines). *Newsweek* or *Time* might review a movie related to disability (e.g., *Wonder* [2017]).

Time: For students, less than 1 hour to find a story; about 30 minutes to read story and reflect on questions. Time in class for discussion: allow 30 minutes.

Possible Outcomes: There will inevitably be one student who insists that no story on disability could be found. But the fact that all classmates found a story challenges this, and you don't have to say much (but can give it zero points). The other thing to watch for is that students will think the stories are just fine, even when they depict pity, charity, or tragic views of disability or when the story is "inspirational" (e.g., high school football player with autism spectrum disorder is treated as "just one of the team").

Talking Points: What section of the paper was the story in, and what page: Was it front page news, in the lifestyle section, or small article buried on page 7? Was it the lighter side of the news or an inspirational story? Was it a review of a movie or TV show, and was disability a main point or an aside? What language was used? That is, was it person-first language (e.g., person with a disability"), or "patient" for people in the community, or "disabled people" lumped as one group, or very emotive words like "afflicted" or "suffers from" or "wheelchair bound"?

Grading Rubric: Like other activities in this chapter, it is best if this is either ungraded or else given all points for completion without regard to quality.

Handout: 3.4: Instructions for Students.

Additional Reading

ADA National Network. *Guidelines for writing about people with disabilities*. https://adata.org/factsheet/ADANN-writing

Mellifont, D. (2017). Hold your traditional discourses! A study exploring newspaper and web news reporting of New York's inaugural disability pride parade. *Asia Pacific Media Educator, 27*(1). http://journals.sagepub.com/doi/abs/10.1177/1326365X17701793 (freeabstract)

National Center on Journalism and Disability. *Disability language style guide*. http://ncdj.org/style-guide/

National Disability Rights Network. *Reporting and writing about disabilities*. (ndrn.org or organization or for guidelines go to: https://www.ndrn.org/images/Documents/Advocacy/Amicus_Activity/Guidelines_for_Reporting_and_Writing_about_People_with_Disabilities.pdf)

Handout 3.4: Instructions for Students

A. Find a newspaper or TV or online news story from the past 6 months about a person with a disability. (If you go online for this, make sure you find out the context for the story: Where did it appear? On what page? What search words located the story? What was the source?) *Note*: You may use *Time*, *Newsweek*, or other national or local magazines.

B. Copy/print the article to bring to class.

C. Answer the following questions and be prepared to discuss them in class:

1. What section of the paper was the story in and on what page: Was it front-page news, in the lifestyle section, or in a small article buried on page 7? If on TV, when did it come on in the program? Was it the lighter side of the news or an "inspirational" story?
2. What was the purpose of the article/story?
3. What was the writer's/presenter's perspective on disability?
4. Were the words of the person with a disability liberally quoted, that is, was the disabled person's perspective reflected in the story?
5. What effect was the story meant to have on readers/listeners? What effect did it have on you?
6. Did hearing about the news stories of other students lead you to rethink anything?

Activity 3.5: The Economics of Disability

Activity: Exploring the bidirectional relations between disability and poverty.

Where: Online and class discussion.

Purpose: To understand that (a) disability and poverty are very related in that each increases the likelihood of the other, although rates differ across the United States, and (b) rates of attention deficit hyperactivity disorder (ADHD) and learning disabilities in grades K–12 follow the money, such that more children are diagnosed in counties with higher average incomes.

Learning Objectives

1. To investigate the rates of disability across the United States.
2. To compare rates of disability and rates of poverty across the United States.
3. To examine the disability, poverty, ADHD, and learning disability rates in one state (where the student lives or is from).
4. To find current information (past 3 years) about the relation between income and disability.

Materials: Handout 3.5, plus each student will either email in advance or come with a one-page handout for each member of the class to be used in discussion.

Preparation: For this assignment, have students use the state or territory where they were born or, if from outside the United States or territories, the state in which they are attending school.

Time: 1 hour on Internet, 45–60 minutes for class sharing and discussion.

Possible Outcomes: If students have difficulties finding current articles, Google Scholar (https://scholar.google.com) is a good place to start, setting the time frame for the past 3 years. If they are having trouble seeing the connection between income and disability, in class do a comparison of, say, Connecticut (a high-income state) and Arkansas (a low-income state) for poverty and for disability; results would illustrate a clear connection between the two.

Talking Points: Disability is a social construction and is created in part by a mismatch between the abilities of a person and the environment. Income levels, health insurance, and access to quality healthcare are important parts of that environment. The difference in rates of disability between the higher and lower income states is quite dramatic. In addition, the likelihood of having less generous government (vs.

private or employer-based) insurance is higher for those with disabilities. Children with disabilities are more likely to be living alone with a single mother and below the poverty line. A map of the United States shows the highest rates of both poverty and disability in the Southeast, but just seeing the relation is not the end point; discussion could include social justice values and implications for policy.

Grading Rubric: 2 points for A, 2 points for B, 3 points for C in Handout 3.5a.

Handout: 3.5a: Instructions for Students; 3.5b: Handout for Class Discussion When Students Bring in Their Findings.

Additional Reading

Brault, M. W. (2012). Americans with disabilities: 2010. *Current Population Reports, 7*, 1–131.

Braithwaite, J., & Mont, D. (2009). Disability and poverty: A survey of World Bank poverty assessments and implications. *ALTER-European Journal of Disability Research/Revu Européenne de Recherche sur le Handicap, 3*(3), 219–232.

Chapman, C., Laird, J., Ifill, N., & Ramani, K. (2011). *Trends in high school dropout and completion rates in the United States: 1972—2009* (Compendium report. NCEW 2012–006). Washington, DC: National Center for Education Statistics.

Christle, C. A., Jolivete, K., & Nelson, C. M. (2007). School characteristics related to high school dropout rates. *Remedial and Special Education, 28*(6), 325–339.

DeBerard, M. S., Spielmans, G. I., & Julka, D. L. (2004). Predictors of academic achievement and retention among college freshmen: A longitudinal study. *College Student Journal, 38*(1), 66.

Dunn, C., Chambers, D., & Rabren, K. (2004). Variables affecting students' decisions to drop out of school. *Remedial and Special Education, 25*(5) 314–332.

Emmett, T. (2005). Disability and poverty. In E. Alant & L. L. Loyd (Eds.), *Augmentative and alternative communication interventions: Beyond poverty* (pp. 68–94). London: Whurr.

Fitzgerald, E. (2007). Disability and poverty. In C. Mel (Ed.), *Welfare policy and poverty* (p. 229). Dublin: Institute of Public Administration and Combat Poverty Agency.

Fujiura, G. T., & Yamaki, K. (2000). Trends in demography of childhood poverty and disability. *Exceptional Children, 66*(2), 187–199.

Grech, S. (2011). Poverty and disability. *Disability & Society, 26*(7), 888–891.

Huang, J. (2011). Work disability, mortgage default, and life satisfaction in the economic downturn: Evidence from the Panel Study of Income Dynamics. *Journal of Disability Policy Studies, 22*(4), 237–246.

Jorgensen, S., Ferraro, V., Fichten, C., & Havel, A. (2009). Predicting college retention and dropout: Sex and disability. https://files.eric.ed.gov/fulltext/ED505873.pdf

Leone, P. E., Christle, C. A., Nelson, C. M., Skiba, R., Frey, A., & Jolivette, K. (2003). *School failure, race, and disability: Promoting positive outcomes, decreasing vulnerability for involvement with the juvenile justice system.* Washington, DC: National Center on Education, Disability, and Juvenile Justice.

Olkin, R. (2017). *Disability-affirmative therapy: A case formulation template for clients with disabilities.* New York: Oxford University Press.

Palmer, M. (2011). Disability and poverty: A conceptual review. *Journal of Disability Policy Studies, 21*(4), 210–218.

Robertson, C. T., Egelhof, R., & Hoke, M. (2008). Get sick, get out: The medical causes of home mortgage foreclosures. *Health Matrix: Journal of Law-Medicine, 18*(1), 65–104.

Scanlon, D., & Mellard, D. F. (2002). Academic and participation profiles of school-age dropouts with and without disabilities. *Exceptional Children, 68*(2), 239–258.

Thurlow, M. L., Sinclair, M. F., & Johnson, D. R. (2002). Students with disabilities who drop out of school: Implications for policy and practice. *Issue Brief: Examining Current Challenges in Secondary Education and Transition, 1*(2). https://files.eric.ed.gov/fulltext/ED468582.pdf

Wagner, M. M., & Blackorby, J. (1996). Transition from high school to work or college: How special education students fare. *Special Education for Students with Disabilities, 6*(1), 103–120.

Wagner, M., Newman, L., Cameto, R., Garza, N., & Levine, P. (2005). *After high school: A first look at the postschool experiences of youth with disabilities.* A report from the National Longitudinal Transition Study-2 (NLTS2). SRI Project #P11182. https://files.eric.ed.gov/fulltext/ED494935.pdf

Handout 3.5a: Instructions for Students

A. Go online to find a map of rates of poverty across the United States. Then locate a map of rates of disabilities across the United States. Compare the two maps: What do you notice?

B. Go online and find a map of income levels for the state (or U.S. territory) in which you were born (or, if not from the United States, the state in which you are attending school). The map should show counties. Now find a map of the rates of ADHD and learning disabilities by county for the same state (or territory). What do you notice?

C. Find a current (past 3 years) article on the relation between disability and income and list its main findings. Make a one-page handout (or PowerPoint) to email or bring to class, a copy for each student and instructor.

Handout 3.5b: Handout for Class Discussion When Students Bring in Their Findings

The following is an excerpt from Olkin (2017).

> Disability and poverty are inextricably linked (Braithwaite & Mont, 2009; Emmett, 2005; Fitzgerald, 2007; Palmer, 2011). People with disabilities are much more likely than those without disabilities to live below the poverty line, to have government (versus private) insurance or no insurance, to have lower household incomes than their neighbors, and to be unemployed or underemployed. Chronic illness and work disability account for about half the defaults on mortgages (Huang, 2011; Robertson et al, 2008). Poverty is a risk factor for dropping out of high school (Chapman et al, 2011). The data on disability as a risk factor for dropout mostly shows a higher rate of dropout (Dunn et al, 2004; Leone et al, 2003; Scanlon & Mallard, 2002; Thurlow et al., 2002). Additionally, disability is associated with poverty and thus with more precarious school districts, both of which are risk factors for high school dropout (Chapman et al., 2011; Christle et al, 2007). Fewer students with disabilities attend college (Wagner & Blackorby, 1996; Wagner et al., 2005). Medical issues and health related quality of life are associated with dropout in college (DeBerard et al., 2004; Jorgensen et al., 2009). On the flip side, persons living in poverty are more likely to have disabilities (Fujiura & Yamaki, 2000; Grech, 2011). (Olkin, 2017, p. 128)

Activity 3.6: Intersectionality (Part I; See Chapter 9 for Parts II and III)

Activity: Students will research their assigned disability in the context of their actual gender, sexual orientation, race/ethnicity, age, religion, and national origin.

Where: On computer.

Purpose: To integrate disability into the context of the whole person using their own gender, age, religion, ethnicity, national origin, and sexual orientation.

Learning Objectives

1. To relate disability to the context of the whole person.
2. To determine what information about intersectionality is and is not readily available.
3. To compare and contrast insider (person with contextual characteristics) and outsider (person with a specific disability) perspectives.

Materials: Internet and research database access.

Preparation: Assign each person a disability (see Handout 3.6a).

Time: 1.5 hours.

Possible Outcomes: Some students will find lots of information, depending on which disability they were assigned, and others will have trouble finding anything about intersectionality other than perhaps gender and age at onset. But the United States has a national organization for almost every disability, including orphan disabilities (National Organization of Rare Disorders), and that is often the place to start. Students from other countries without much ethnic diversity or developed public healthcare systems might not locate much about race/ethnicity and their disability in their own country.

Talking Points: What information was easy to find? What was hard to find? What conclusions do you draw from what you found and why? Which countries seem to keep excellent records (e.g., Sweden, Norway) and which do not (United States). Which disabilities have more information (e.g., spinal cord injury national registry), and which have much less? Is it based on frequency of disability, population it affects, or something else?

Grading Rubric: 10 points (1 point per question and 1 for discussion)

Handouts: 3.6a: Instructions for Teachers; 3.6b: Instructions for Students.

Additional Reading

Meyer, I. H. (2010). Identity, stress, and resilience in lesbians, gay men, and bisexuals of color. *Counseling Psychology, 38*(3), 1–9. https://doi.org/10.1177/0011000009351601

Olkin, R. (2017). Disability-affirmative therapy IV: Context and intersectionality—interplay of disability and other demographic variables. In *Disability-affirmative therapy: A case formulation template for clients with disabilities*. New York: Oxford University Press.

Riddell, S., & Watson, N. (2014). *Disability, culture and identity.* New York: Routledge.

Handout 3.6a: Instructions for Teachers

Using the list of assigned disabilities from Assignment 3.2a (and reproduced below), assign each student a disability (or ask them to keep the one already assigned to them). If you are assigning a disability to students for the first time, remember to keep a few in reserve so that if a student should get his or her own disability, the student can come privately and trade with you. Students will do research on their disability in the context of their own characteristics. Then there are some questions to help guide the discussion (see Talking Points).

Ankylosing spondylitis	Fibromyalgia
Attention deficit hyperactivity disorder, combined type	Little person (dwarfism)
Asthma	Lupus (systemic lupus erythematosus)
Autism	Multiple sclerosis, relapsing and remitting
Blindness	Multiple sclerosis, primary progressive
Bipolar disorder	Osteoarthritis
Cerebral palsy (since this occurs from birth, the person is to imagine that they have never been told much about the disability other than that they "walk funny")	Scleroderma
Chronic obstructive pulmonary disease	Sickle cell disease
Chronic kidney disease	Spinal cord injury (T3 level)
Congenital heart disease (specifically coarctation of the aorta, newly discovered)	Spinal cord injury (C6 level)
Crohn's Disease	Tourette syndrome combined with obsessive-compulsive disorder
Diabetes, insulin dependent	Traumatic brain injury (from explosion, but no brain penetration)
Epilepsy	Turner syndrome
	Williams syndrome

Handout 3.6b: Instructions for Students

You are a person with various characteristics, such as gender, sexual orientation, race/ethnicity, national origin, religion, age, and socioeconomic status. For this assignment, you were assigned a specific disability (or you were asked to keep the same diagnosis for the whole course).

For this assignment, you will be researching your assigned disability, using your own characteristics. What can you find on your disability as it intersects with your other features? Then, what can you find about intersectionality—your disability and many of your features all at once? After you complete the form, come to class prepared to discuss what you have learned.

Fill in the form below:

		About Me	What I Found Out About (Me) + (My Disability)
1	Gender		
2	Race/ethnicity(ies)		
3	Sexual orientation		
4	National origin		
5	Age		
6	Religion		
7	Socioeconomic status		
8	Financial and social safety net		
9	Intersectionality: me plus at least 2 of the above		
10	Anything else?		

4 Hearing from Insiders

SO OFTEN WE see and hear about disability through the lens of a professional or writer who is not disabled; this distorts the content and message. In this chapter, the lived experiences of disabled people are explored. Two activities use documentaries; in one activity students interview a person with a disability using an interview protocol. For each activity, it is helpful to encourage students to share their honest emotional and cognitive reactions, both initially and then after the assignments. A simple set of two statements can help them record their thoughts and emotions:

Right now I feel...
My first thought is...

Teaching Disability. Rhoda Olkin, Oxford University Press. © Oxford University Press 2021.
DOI: 10.1093/oso/9780190850661.003.0004

Activity 4.1: *King Gimp*: Academy Award–Winning Documentary

Activity: Watch the documentary *King Gimp* (1999; directed by Susan Hannah Hadary and William A. Whiteford) and respond to questions. The documentary follows the life of Dan Keplinger from the age of 12 to 25, when he graduates from college with an art degree.

Where: It is recommended to watch this in class, as students may not have access to the film (e.g., it is on HBO). Discussion should be in class.

Purpose: To hear directly from a person with a significant disability; to see what is possible in life given appropriate accommodations and supports.

Learning Objectives

1. To gain awareness of how one's reactions to Dan's look and speech change over the course of the film.
2. To be able to cite several actions of a strong advocate (in this case the mother) for a child with a disability.
3. To identify specific actions that teachers take that can discourage or encourage students with disabilities.

Materials: Video/DVD of *King Gimp* (film is subtitled) and Handout 4.1.

Preparation: None, but it is highly recommended that students have watched and discussed the film *My Left Foot* prior to this. Both that film and this documentary are about a man with significant cerebral palsy; both men go into the arts. Comparing the two films—one a fictionalized version of a real life, the other a documentary—is useful.

Time: 39 minutes to watch the film and 30 minutes to discuss.

Possible Outcomes: Often students are initially alarmed when the documentary begins, and they cannot understand Dan's speech. Then the subtitles come on, and they feel relief. This can be a useful point of discussion. Over the course of the documentary, Dan becomes more of a whole person and not just a disability. But students may still be caught up in the physical issues facing Dan in everyday life and need help understanding that educational and attitudinal barriers were the major obstacles for him. In addition, some may feel hesitant to talk about Dan's romantic and sexual feelings and have trouble seeing these as fundamental rights of people with disabilities.

Talking Points: Dan initially lives alone with his single mother. This is a more common family configuration for children with disabilities than for children without disabilities—What are the implications of this? The mother believes that Dan is intelligent, and she fights very hard for Dan to attend school and get the accommodations he needs. What might have happened differently if she had not been able to advocate for him so effectively? Why might the father have left? Note the power of teachers—one teacher who is very discouraging and another who is flexible in his art assignments to take Dan's limitations into account. Dan develops a crush on one of his assistants; discuss her role in his life from her perspective and his perspective. What are possible options for Dan's sexual expression?

Grading Rubric: No grade.

Handout: 4.1: Instructions for Students.

Additional Reading

Chen, K., Tseng, M., Shieh, J., Lu Lu, & Huang, C. (2014). Determinants of quality of life in children with cerebral palsy: A comprehensive biopsychosocial approach. *Research in Developmental Disabilities, 35*(2), 520–528.

Hadary, S. H., & Whiteford, W. A. (Directors). (1999). *King Gimp.* College Park, MD: University of Maryland, Tapestry International, Whiteford-Hadary Productions; HBO.

Kaufman, M., Silverberg, C., & Odette, F. (2003). *The ultimate guide to sex and disability.* San Francisco: Cleis Press.

Mona, L. R. (2003). Sexual options for people with disabilities: Using personal assistance services for sexual expression. *Women & Therapy, 26,* 211–220.

Oskoui, M., Coutinho, F., Dykeman, J., Jette, N., & Pringsheim, T. (2013). An update on the prevalence of cerebral palsy: A systematic review and meta-analysis. *Developmental Medicine and Child Neurology, 55*(6), 509–519.

Shuttleworth, R., & Mona, L. R. (2002). Disability and sexuality: Toward a focus on sexual access. *Disability Studies Quarterly, 22*(4), 2–3.

Handout 4.1: Instructions for Students

Read this list of questions before watching the documentary *King Gimp*. After you watch the film, revisit these questions prior to class discussion. However, discussion does not need to be limited to these questions.

Questions

1. What were your initial emotional and cognitive reactions to Dan? How did those change over time, if at all?
2. What role did Dan's mother play in getting him into a regular school?
3. There was a teacher who discouraged Dan from doing art. Did you at least partly agree with that teacher?
4. There was another teacher who changed his assignments in a very creative way. In your field of study, are there assignments that lend themselves to being flexible and those that do not? What changes might be made? Do these changes alter the fundamental character of the assignments?
5. Dan was frustrated in his romantic and sexual feelings with no outlets for either. How might you talk with him about these areas as a (a) friend or (b) peer counselor or (c) therapist.
6. If you watched *My Left Foot*, find the ways the two depictions are similar and how they are different.
7. Could Dan have played the role of Christy Brown in *My Left Foot*? Why or why not?

Activity 4.2: Interviewing a Person with a Disability

Activity: Students will use a protocol (RESPECTFUL: **R**eligion/spirituality, **E**conomic background, **S**exual identity, **P**ersonal style/education, **E**thnic/racial identity, **C**hronology/life span, **T**rauma, **F**amily background, **U**nique physical characteristics, **L**ocation of residence and language) to interview a person with a hidden or visible disability.

Where: The interview should be conducted in a safe but somewhat private space (e.g., a room in a library; a corner table in a café). The report can be written online. There are potential add-ons to the assignment (see Handout 4.2c) for home and in class.

Purpose: To interact directly with a person with a disability and to conduct an interview that puts the disability into a context of a whole person.

Learning Objectives

1. To learn how to use a protocol to conduct an interview.
2. To recognize contextual factors related to disability in an individual.
3. To compare their interview with that of a classmate.

Materials: Handout 4.2a: Instructions for Students; 4.2b: Interview Protocol; 4.2c: Instructions for Teachers—Possible Additions to the Assignment.

Preparation: Students should be given some guidelines on how to find and select a person to interview (see Handout 4.2a). Also, they should be told explicitly to safeguard all interview materials (any notes, reports, tape recordings) as they would any confidential material (i.e., password-protected file in a password-protected computer; in a secure location behind at least one lock [door, file cabinet]). No names or identifying information should be used in written materials.

Time: Approximately 3–4 hours—to find person to interview, set up meeting, conduct interview, and write a report. Add-ons will take additional time.

Possible Outcomes: A student may ask to conduct the interview by telephone, Skype, or Zoom. However, one goal of the interview is to interact directly with a person with a disability. Online video and telephone allow some distancing of interlocutors and have a different (limiting) impact on the interviewer. I suggest insisting on face-to-face interviews. If a student says that no one with a disability could be located, remind the student of the wide range of disabilities (asthma, diabetes, hearing loss, learning disabilities, depression, etc.) and the very unlikely case of not knowing anyone with a disability.

Talking Points: There is an expression in rehabilitation that if you know one person with a disability, you know *one* person with a disability. Therefore, this activity is made more meaningful by sharing the interviews across students. Care should be taken not to overgeneralize from one disability to a different disability, from one person to another. (See instructions for add-ons in Handout 4.2c.)

Grading Rubric: 15 points possible, using the following rubric for grading:

12–15 points = A (follows all directions and includes all required parts at expected level of education and writing; draws appropriate conclusions from interview data; presents information clearly)
9–11 points = B (follows all directions but one part is below expected educational level; draws only obvious conclusions from data; information could be more clearly presented)
<9 points = C or below (does not follow all directions and/or more than one part is below expected level; conclusions are perfunctory and/or not clearly connected to data; information not clearly presented)

Handouts: 4.2a: Instructions for Students; 4.2b: Interview Protocol; 4.2c: Instructions for Teachers—Possible Additions to the Assignment.

Additional Reading

Brayboy, B. M., & Deyhle, D. (2000). Insider-outsider: Researchers in American Indian communities. *Theory Into Practice, 39*(3), 163–169.

Caldwell, K. (2013). Dyadic interviewing: A technique valuing interdependence in interviews with individuals with intellectual disabilities. *Qualitative Research, 14*(4), 1–20.

Chen, X. M. (1997). "Insider" and "outsider" in qualitative research. *Sociological Studies, 6*, 80–89.

Cui, K. (2014). The insider-outsider role of a Chinese researcher doing fieldwork in China: The implications of cultural context. *Qualitative Social Work, 14*(3), 356–369.

Lesseliers, J., Van Hove, G., & Vandevelde, S. (2009). Regranting identity to the outgraced: Narratives of persons with learning disabilities: Methodological considerations. *Disability & Society, 24*(4), 411–423.

Polkinghorne, D. E. (2007). Validity issues in narrative research. *Qualitative Inquiry, 13*(4), 471–486.

Sunderland, N., Chenoweth, L., Matthews, N., & Ellem, K. (2014). 1000 voices: Reflective online multimodal narrative inquiry as a research methodology for disability research. *Qualitative Social Work, 14*(1), 48–64.

Handout 4.2a: Instructions for Students

1. Find someone *with a chronic health condition or disability* to interview for about 30–45 minutes. (It may be a student, even one in your class. It may be a family member. It may *not* be a current or former client. *Do* use a pseudonym for the interviewee.)
2. Find a safe but semiprivate space to conduct the interview (i.e., do not meet a stranger in either of your homes). Suggestions include a room at a library, a corner table in a quiet café, a park, a room at a church/synagogue/mosque/temple.
3. Conduct the interview using the Interview Protocol below.
4. Write a report on your interview using the protocol as a guide. Then draw conclusions about the interface between the person's chronic health condition or disability and the person's other demographics and culture.

Handout 4.2b: Interview Protocol

1. Please tell me a little about yourself. I'd like to know about your gender identity, age, race/ethnicity, national origin or part of United States where you grew up, religion, sexual orientation, socioeconomic status growing up and now, level of education.
2. Can you tell me about your chronic health condition or disability (how acquired, what words are used to describe it, what functional limitations there are, any assistive technology used)?
3. What *five* words would you use to describe your identity, in order of importance?
4. What is your employment history? Future prospects?
5. Compared to most people your age, including people who do not have a chronic health condition or disability, what do you consider your level of power and privilege, and why? (*Note*: Could use scale of 1–100, then ask for explanation.)
6. RESPECTFUL: **R**eligion/spirituality, **E**conomic background, **S**exual identity, **P**ersonal style/education, **E**thnic/racial identity, **C**hronology/life span, **T**rauma, **F**amily background, **U**nique physical characteristics, **L**ocation of residence and language.
7. Best and worst thing about having your chronic health condition/disability.

Writing Your Report: Use the following headers to complete your report. (No names or identifying information of the interviewee should be used in written materials.) The final results will be two to three pages.

Identifying Information: A few sentences saying who the person is (e.g., 35-year-old White male with cerebral palsy, a full-time student. Heterosexual, never married, lives with roommates, has new girlfriend of 3 months).

Chronic Health Condition/Disability: What is it and what words did the person use to describe it; what are the functional limitations; any assistive technology used; effects on relationships or other details learned in interview.

Chosen Identity: Their *five* words of "identity."

Respectful: **R**eligion/spirituality; **E**conomic background; **S**exual identity; **P**ersonal style/education; **E**thnic/racial identity; **C**hronology/life span; **T**rauma; **F**amily background; **U**nique physical characteristics; **L**ocation of residence and language.

Best and Worst Thing About Having a Chronic Health Condition/Disability: Use the person's own words here as much as possible.

Conclusions: One or two paragraphs on how the chronic health condition/disability and other variables interact for this person (i.e., a cultural formulation). Include factors of coping, support, and resilience.

Handout 4.2c: Instructions for Teachers—Possible Additions to the Assignment

1. Have students pair up in class and read each other's interview reports. Then have them note overlaps and contrasts between their own and that of their partner before joining the full class discussion.
2. Have students post their interviews online prior to class and ask them to read all of the interviews prior to class discussion.
3. Make a list across all interviews of the best thing about having a chronic health condition/disability and a list of the worst things. (In all likelihood, many will list the worst thing as prejudice, stigma, discrimination, being asked personal questions all the time, intrusive/inquisitive other people. These are the most common responses by people with disabilities, but often not what outsiders—those without disability—would predict.)

Activity 4.3: Disability in the Family System

Activity: Watch the academy award–winning documentary *Best Boy* (1979; director Ira Wohl; International Film Exchange) and analyze the role of disability in the family using a guide sheet. (See trailer at https://www.youtube.com/watch?v=-MXX14L06nA.)

Where: At home or in class.

Purpose: Disability in a child, sibling, or parent affects the whole family, not just the individual with the disability. However, the effects are not static, as individuals in the family age and health issues affect others. This documentary, produced by a cousin, is an inside look at a family with an adult son with an intellectual disability. It is an intimate portrait of changes within the family as the parents age; the mother grapples with what will happen to her son when she is no longer able to care for him, and the son embarks on a new chapter in his life. The portrayal is warm and intimate and shows the tremendous love within the family.

Learning Objectives

1. List the changes in the family over the 3 years depicted in the documentary.
2. Explain the roles of each member of the family. Did they change over time?
3. Predict what will happen to Philly in the next 5 years as the mother ages.
4. Create a portrait of the family dynamics using a guideline in Handout 4.3.
5. Analyze your own reactions to the family at the beginning and by the end of the documentary.

Materials: Handout with guide to family functioning.

Preparation: None.

Time: 1 hour, 51 minutes to watch the documentary, about 1.5 hours to complete the handout.

Possible Outcomes: Students have found this documentary very affecting and have cited it as very powerful in modifying their view of intellectual disability. However, it is possible that some students experience increased fears about having someone with a disability, specifically an intellectual disability, in the extended family. Thus, it can be important to create space for many diverse reactions. Furthermore, the assignment for this module will be easier for those who have had a course on family systems. It may be necessary to go over key terms in Handout 4.3 for those who have not had such a course.

Talking Points: The class could work in groups of three and discuss the following: Suppose you or your partner were pregnant and early testing indicated a high probability of a child with Down syndrome or other cause of intellectual disability. (a) Think about what you would do in this situation. (b) How might you (your partner, your parents, your other children) react? (c) What preparations might you make? Small groups can be encouraged to share with the class, but no one should feel obliged to do so.

Grading Rubric: 10 points total: 6 points for Part A and 4 points for Part B of Handout 4.3.

Handout: 4.3: Instructions for Students.

Additional Reading or Viewing

Guralnick, M. J. (2016). Early intervention for children with disabilities: An update. *Journal of Applied Research in Intellectual Disabilities, 30*(2), 211–229. https://doi.org/10.1111/jar.12233

McConnell, D., Feldman, M., & Aunos, M. (2017). Parents and parenting with intellectual disabilities: An expanding field of research [Editorial]. *Journal of Applied Research in Intellectual Disabilities, 30*(3), 419–422. https://doi.org/10.1111/jar.12362

Pryce, L., Tweed, A., Hilton, A., & Priest, H. (2015). Tolerating uncertainty: Perceptions of the future for ageing parent caregivers and their adult children with intellectual disabilities. *Journal of Applied Research in Intellectual Disabilities, 30*(1), 84–96. https://doi.org/10.1111/jar.12221

Stott, J., Charlesworth, G., & Scior, K. (2017). Measures of readiness for cognitive behavioural therapy in people with intellectual disability: A systematic review. *Research in Developmental Disabilities, 60*, 37–51. https://doi.org/10.1016/j.ridd.2016.11.003

Wohl, I. (Director and writer). (1979). *Best boy* [Film; documentary]. Los Angeles area: Only Child Motion Pictures.

Wohl, I. (Director and writer). (1997). *Best man:* Best boy *and all of us, 20 years later* [Film; documentary]. New York: New Video Group.

Handout 4.3: Instructions for Students

Part A: Guidelines for analyzing the family: Use the following prompts to write one page on the family system depicted in *Best Boy*. (6 points)

Roles of each member;
Family and individual life stages;
Rules governing the family dynamics;
Supports to the family;
Coping mechanisms;
Risks and vulnerabilities;
Family culture; family system: hierarchy, alliances, boundaries.

Part B: Add a paragraph about your own responses to the documentary and whether you felt it changed you in any way (or not) and why (or why not). (4 points)

5 Laws and How They Affect the Everyday Lives of People with Disabilities

ACTIVITIES IN THIS section shift the focus from the people with disabilities to the systems that affect them and their daily lives and how those systems either help or hinder. Conceptual issues are examined in Activities 5.1–5.3. The burden placed on disabled people in accessing goods and services is highlighted in Activity 5.4.

Teaching Disability. Rhoda Olkin, Oxford University Press. © Oxford University Press 2021.
DOI: 10.1093/oso/9780190850661.003.0005

Activity 5.1: How Laws Affect Everyday Life

Activity: Explore the relations between laws and their direct effects on *your* life.

Purpose: Various laws have great impact on the lives of different groups. The goal of this assignment is to have students find a federal or state law that directly affects their lives. The law should not be a general one that affects all people (e.g., laws against murder, drug use, and burglary) but rather one that speaks directly to certain groups. Several examples may need to be discussed in class first (e.g., the voting rights act, *Brown v. Board of Education of Topeka, Kansas*; the Supreme Court ruling on gay marriage; Oregon's Aid in Dying law; the California proposition that barred affirmative action), and it should be noted that the law may positively or negatively affect certain groups.

Where: On computer or at the library.

Learning objectives

1. Describe a law and all of its main tenets.
2. Explain who supported and who was against the law and why and the process of getting the law passed.
3. Apply the law to your own life and analyze what you believe is different for you because this law was passed.
4. Create a revision to this law that you believe would strengthen it (if it is a positive impact) or weaken it (if it is a negative impact), without simply repealing the law.

Materials: Handout 5.1.

Preparation: Give students an example in class. This will help convey the close relation of a law and those affected by the law. *One example* might be the Education for All Handicapped Children Act of 1975 (reauthorized as the Individuals with Disabilities Education Act). At the time this law was passed, approximately one million children with disabilities were not in any educational setting. The law is a rare example of bipartisan support. Promised federal funding of 25% never materialized, making this an "unfunded mandate" to states, which has caused pushback from poorer states and those who believe states' rights are paramount. Some states put a cap on the number of children with disabilities that can be "found." However, the law has meant individual education plans and reasonable accommodations (RAs) for millions of children.

Time: 30 minutes in class for the example, 2 hours on homework.

Possible Outcomes: Women and minority group members often find this assignment easier than will straight, able-bodied, White males. Laws often target protected classes. However, some state laws or court cases seek to overturn perceived advantages of minority groups (e.g., *Bakke v. Regents of the University of California–Davis Medical School, 1978*, which disallowed affirmative action in admissions). Another possibility might be a law that targets students or mental health professionals. Thus, instructors should not accept "There isn't a law relevant to me" as a viable excuse.

Talking Points: Why did women and minority members find it easier to locate a relevant law? Which laws were designed to have a positive impact on the lives of one or more minority group members? Which laws took away rights? Who was for/against the laws? Were the two sides based on political party (Democrat or Republican) or some other factor (e.g., religion, ethnic group)? What law would the students like to see passed that would be of the greatest benefit to most?

Grading Rubric: 40% of grade based on finding and describing the relevant law, 40% on describing the effect of the law on the student's life, and 20% on what revisions to the law are suggested.

Handout: 5.1: Instructions for Students.

Additional Reading

Crowley, J. S., Nevins, G. R., & Thompson, M. (2015). The Americans with Disabilities Act and HIV/AIDS discrimination: Unfinished business. *Journal of the American Medical Association, 314*(3), 227–228. https://doi.org/10.1001/jama.2015.6637

Dinerstein, R. (2015). *Promises kept, promises broken, promises deferred: The Americans with Disabilities Act. Impact* (American University, WCL Research Paper No. 2016-12). https://ssrn.com/abstract=2750182

Hajnal, Z., Kuk, J., & Lajevardi, N., (2018). We all agree: Strict voter ID laws disproportionately burden minorities. *Journal of Politics, 80*(3). https://www.journals.uchicago.edu/doi/abs/10.1086/696617

Valentino, N., & Neuner, F. G. (2016). Why the sky didn't fall: Mobilizing anger in reaction to voter ID laws. *Political Psychology, 38*(2), 331–350. https://doi.org/10.1111/pops.12332

Handout 5.1: Instructions for Students

Purpose: The purpose of this assignment is to have you explore the relations between a specific law and the direct effects of this law on *your* life. The law may be federal, state, county, or passed by proposition. The law may have enhanced your life in some way or may have hindered you. For example, a local ordinance on "visiting rights" that mandated that houses being renovated must make their entrances accessible would mean that a person in a wheelchair could visit neighbors (e.g., as in Austin, TX). Conversely, when California passed Proposition 8 in 2008, it prohibited same-sex marriage.

Part A: Find a law that directly affects your life. Please do not pick a law that affects everyone mostly equally, such as prohibitions on murder, burglary, drunk driving, legalization of marijuana, raising (or lowering) the driving age, seatbelt laws, and more. The goal is to find a law that targets your demographic and identity specifically. State when the law passed and describe the main tenets of the law. Explain who supported and who was against the law and why and the process of getting the law passed.

Part B: Describe the effects of this law on your life. Apply the law to your own life and analyze what you believe is different for you because this law was passed.

Part C: Create a revision to this law that you believe would strengthen it (if it is a positive impact) or weaken it (if it is a negative impact) without simply repealing the law.

Activity 5.2: About Segregation: Is Separate Ever Equal?

Activity: This activity explores segregation. Students will find places in the real world where people with disabilities are separated from those without disabilities.

Where: Out in the world.

Purpose: In the famous Supreme Court case of *Brown v. Board of Education of Topeka, Kansas, 1954*, psychologists testified that segregation had been shown to cause deleterious psychoemotional effects on those segregated, and the court ruled that "separate" could not be "equal." Nonetheless, segregation has essentially been codified in law for those with disabilities—by making places and activities accessible, the accessible portion may be separate from others. Although there are no longer signs saying "colored" and "white," there are signs with wheelchair logos designating separate areas for persons with particular disabilities.

Learning Objectives

1. List places that segregate people with disabilities from those without disabilities. (50%)
2. Describe the settings in which people with disabilities are partially or wholly segregated. (Part of the 50% for Objective 1)
3. Go to or utilize the segregated area and describe your experience. (20%)
4. Analyze the rationale and the practical necessity for segregation of people with disabilities. (20%)
5. Prepare a report on alternatives that would minimize segregation of people with disabilities. (10%)

Materials: Handout, tracking form.

Preparation: Students need some background for this assignment. Everyone should be familiar with the main arguments in *Brown v. Board of Education of Topeka, Kansas*. They need some familiarity with the tenets of "reasonable accommodations (RA)." Showing a documentary or film depicting the segregated South and/or a documentary on internment of Japanese Americans during World War II (an extreme example of segregation) can be a useful preamble to this assignment. In-class discussion of when students felt excluded or ostracized can help set a framework. It is strongly suggested that students watch and discuss in class: *Isn't it a pity? The real problem with special needs* (2015; T. Dunlap, TED Talk [Video]. https://www.youtube.com/watch?v=UJ7QaCFbizo).

Time: Variable; students can be asked to track this during their week.

Possible Outcomes: It is suggested that students be given a full week on this assignment because some students may have initial difficulty "seeing" segregation. For example, they may see a designated seating area in a movie theater and think of it as an accommodation (which it is) and overlook that it also segregates wheelchair users. Furthermore, the focus may initially be on wheelchair users, and other types of segregation for different disabilities will be overlooked (which is why one example given on Handout 6.2 is about hearing impairments).

Talking Points: Various disability laws require RAs, and that the person with the disability be involved in the process of deciding on RAs. Further, the result must be an RA that works. However, these laws do not require an entity to choose the RA that the person with a disability requests or the one that is most desirable. Thus, accommodations may be segregating. For example, suppose entering a lunchroom requires a person to go down a few steps with no ramp, and an employee who uses a wheelchair requests an RA to eat with colleagues. The RA could involve setting up an accessible table at the top of the few steps, with room for colleagues and a wheelchair user. The table is within sight of the other tables in the lunch area, but not actually among those tables. It is possible that the wheelchair user would arrive at the accessible table and all colleagues would be at the inaccessible tables. Further, suppose a drink machine is in the inaccessible area. The RA could be that the person with a disability is to ask a secretary to go get the drink for him or her ("a favor") rather than being allowed to get it independently. These accommodations "work" in the sense that they provide an accessible lunch area and a means to get a drink from the machine, but students should see the downside of these RAs. Students can discuss the differences among the concepts of accommodation, integration, and inclusion.

Students in the class may have examples of segregation that they have encountered, perhaps on a daily basis. They can be encouraged to share those examples, but they should not feel obligated to do so. One important point for the class to grasp is that their current and future clients with disabilities encounter segregation every day, and this has psychological and interpersonal repercussions; not all clients will be equally aware of these repercussions.

Grading Rubric: See Learning Objectives for suggested weighting for grades.

Handout: 5.2: Instructions for Students.

Additional Reading and Viewing

MOVIES OR DOCUMENTARIES

History Channel. (2018, October). *Japanese-American internment during WWII* [Video]. YouTube. https://www.youtube.com/watch?v=cZTioTkHcBo

Icard, R. (2016). *Segregation is back* (TV documentary).

Kodama, B. (Producer and director). (2016). *One-two-one-seven: A story of Japanese internment* [Video].

TED. (2014, April 22). *Disabling segregation | Dan Habib* [Video]. YouTube. https://www.youtube.com/watch?v=izkN5vLbnw8)

Baker, S. K. (Writer and director). (2003). *With all deliberate speed: The legacy of* Brown v. Board.

ARTICLES

Clark, K. B., Chein, I., & Cook, S. W. (2004). The effects of segregation and the consequences of desegregation: A (September, 1952) social science statement in the *Brown v. Board of Education of Topeka* Supreme Court case. *American Psychologist, 59*(6), 495–501. http://dx.doi.org/10.1037/0003-066X.59.6.495

Cregan, C., Kulik, C. T., & Bainbridge, H. T. J. (2016). Differences in well-being among people with disabilities in paid employment: Level of restriction, gender and labour market context. *Social Policy Administration, 51*(7), 1210–1230. https://doi.org/10.1111/spol.12263

Phuong Do, D., Frank, R., & Iceland, J. (2017). Black-White metropolitan segregation and self-rated health: Investigating the role of neighborhood poverty. *Social Science & Medicine, 187*, 85–92. https://doi.org/10.1016/j.socscimed.2017.06.010

Quillian, L. (2017). Segregation as a source of contextual advantage: A formal theory with application to American cities. *Russell Sage Foundation Journal of the Social Sciences, 39*(2), 152–169.

Handout 5.2: Instructions for Students

The goal of this assignment is to evaluate current situations that segregate people with disabilities, such as a separate entrance than that used by people without disabilities; a public transit system of linked trains/cars with only some designated as accessible; a separate bathroom or stall; eating places with accessible locations away from the mainstream.

For this assignment, there are four steps:

1. Spend 1 week observing and listing places that segregate people with disabilities from those without disabilities. *See Sample Tracking Form and an example.*
2. Analyze the rationale and the practical necessity for segregation of people with disabilities. (Example: Only one stall was large enough for a wheelchair and had handrails; making all stalls sufficiently large would cut down the total number of stalls. However, all stalls could have handrails.) Show the rationale/necessity on your tracking form.
3. Go to or utilize the segregated area and describe your experience on the tracking form.
4. On a separate page, write a report on accessibility alternatives that would minimize segregation of people with disabilities. (Suggested length: ½—1 page)

Sample Tracking Form

Place	Context	How Segregated	Rationale	Experience
Safeway (supermarket)	Checkout lines	Only one line has the "wheelchair" symbol and also an accessible-level payment machine	Lowering all payment machines would make them too short for standing people. But could machines be adjustable height?	Stood on line at accessible checkout even though it was longer than other lines. Resented being forced onto this line.
Safeway (supermarket)	Parking	Designated spots for handicapped parking	Handicapped parking is closest to entrances and wider to allow wheelchairs to get out of the car. This makes sense and is needed.	All spots were taken. Also, if a wheelchair needed to exit on a specific side of the car, there was only one possible space for that car.
TV	News on MSNBC	The captioning was awful and out of synch with the speakers, making it hard for Deaf people to understand the news	Captioning a live show requires real-time typing, and it is hard to keep pace with speakers.	Watching by captioning alone, I felt bewildered at some portions. Also, it was harder to tell nuance such as joking.

Activity 5.3: Distributive Justice

Activity: Engage in thought experiments to find acceptable limits of social justice and distributive justice (as defined in Handout 5.3a).

Where: In class.

Purpose: To illustrate how values such as social or distributive justice translate into everyday life and challenge students to find their own boundaries.

Learning Objectives

1. Engage in thought experiments.
2. Describe own reactions to various situations.
3. Predict differences across students.
4. Utilize contextual factors to understand differences across students and situations.
5. Analyze class results.

Materials: None.

Preparation: First, go over Handout 5.3a in class. Then divide the class into groups of three to four. Have them discuss the three thought experiments (Handout 5.3b), with each person formulating their own answers. Finally, come together as a class and discuss findings.

Time: 1 hour minimum: 10 minutes to discuss the concepts of social versus distributive justice, 30 minutes for small groups to discuss the three thought experiments, and 20 minutes for whole-class discussion.

Possible Outcomes: Some students may claim pure altruism (i.e., that they would always honor the rights of people with disabilities even if it meant giving up something of their own). It can be instructive to push this point. For example, suppose a large group of people with disabilities sat in all the rows at a movie theater so that you had to sit in the first row? Or all the people with disabilities were let into a line at Disneyland so that your wait time increased by half an hour, or an hour, or two? Or a person with a disability got the position you applied for or the promotion you wanted? The point is that everyone does have a limit even if they have not experienced it yet. It is also likely that students who hold a marginalized or stigmatized identity will feel differently and more strongly in favor of "leveling the playing field" than will more mainstream students. Current news events and voting patterns can show how different populations within the United States see things very differently.

Talking Points: (a) When the rights of one group infringe on the rights of another group, how does one decide what is right? Suppose both groups are disadvantaged and stigmatized populations? How does one avoid comparing levels of stigma, discrimination, and prejudice across different groups? (b) If there were a number of people with disabilities who would be advantaged, yet also a number at which the nondisabled would start to object, how might that number be determined so that a balance is struck that seems "fair and equitable"? (c) What does equity mean in the context of disadvantage? (d) Is there such a thing as "reverse discrimination" as might be claimed by the majority group (e.g., the Bakke decision; see Activity 5.1)? (e) Why are most of the additional readings in disciplines other than psychology?

Grading Rubric: None (in-class activity).

Handouts: 5.3a: Social Versus Distributive Justice; 5.3b: Three Thought Experiments.

Additional Reading

Anastasiou, D., Kauffman, J. M., & Michael, D. (2014). Disability in multicultural theory: Conceptual and social justice issues. *Journal of Disability Policy Studies*, *27*(1), 3–12.

Arsenio, W. F. (2015). Moral psychological perspectives on distributive justice and social inequities. *Child Development Perspectives*, *9*(2), 91–95. https://doi.org/10.1111/cdep.12115

Berger, J., Zelditch, M., Anderson, B., Cohen, B. P. (2015). Distributive justice: A status value formulation. http://hdl.handle.net/1969.1/154695

Graybill, E., Baker, C. N., Cloth, A., Fisher, S., & Nastasi, B. K. (2017). An analysis of social justice research in school psychology. *International Journal of School & Educational Psychology*, *6*(2), 77–89. https://doi.org/10.1080/21683603.2017.1302850

Iqbal, M. (2018). Poverty, inequalities and the perceptions on distributive justice. *Journal of King Abdulaziz University: Islamic Economics*, *31*(1). https://ssrn.com/abstract=3183582

Krahn, G., Klein Walker, G., & Correa-De-Araujo, R. (2015). Persons with disabilities as an unrecognized health disparity population. *American Journal of Public Health*, *105*(S2), S198–S206.

Mithen, J., Aitken, Z., Ziersch, A., & Kavanagh, A. M. (2015). Inequalities in social capital and health between people with and without disabilities. *Social Science & Medicine*, *126*, 26–35. https://doi.org/10.1016/j.socscimed.2014.12.009

Perales, F., Baxter, J., & Tai, T. (2015). Gender, justice and work: A distributive approach to perceptions of housework fairness. *Social Science Research*, *51*, 51–63. https://doi.org/10.1016/j.ssresearch.2014.12.010

Pereira, R. H. M., Schwanen, T., & Banister, D. (2016). Distributive justice and equity in transportation. *Transport Reviews*, *37*(2), 170–191. https://doi.org/10.1080/01441647.2016.1257660

Snell, C., Bevan, M., & Thomson, H. (2015). Justice, fuel poverty and disabled people in England. *Energy Research and Social Science*, *10*, 123–132.

Villanueva-Flores, M., Valle, R., & Bornay-Barrachina, M. (2017). Perceptions of discrimination and distributive injustice among people with physical disabilities: In jobs, compensation and career development. *Personnel Review*, *46*(3), 680–698. https://doi.org/10.1108/PR-04-2015-0098

Handout 5.3a: Social Versus Distributive Justice

Social justice involves the distribution of goods equally. A social justice approach to distribution of money would be that everyone received the same amount (equality). In distributive justice, the allocation of money would take into account each person's prior holdings of money and distribute money so that the least advantaged are better off than they would be if distribution were equal. The poorest among the students would get the most, and the richest would get the least. In a more radical form of distributive justice, the richest might give up some of their holdings to balance out those of the poorest. An example is health insurance: The healthiest pay the same as those less healthy, thereby subsidizing the latter. Another example is fire or flood insurance, where those in low-risk areas might pay the same premiums as those in high-risk areas, thereby equalizing payments despite uneven risks. John Rawls wrote:

> Society should be structured so that the greatest possible amount of liberty is given to its members, limited only by the notion that the liberty of any one member shall not infringe upon that of any other member. Secondly, inequalities either social or economic are only to be allowed if the worst off will be better off than they might be under an equal distribution. Finally, if there is such a beneficial inequality, this inequality should not make it harder for those without resources to occupy positions of power, for instance public office. (https://en.wikipedia.org/wiki/A_Theory_of_Justice)

Disability accommodations sometimes involve distributive justice. A simple example is handicapped parking spaces that only people with the required placards/license plates can use and others cannot. Generally, no one seems to mind giving up the closest spaces, until (a) all other nearby spots are taken; (b) there are separate areas for handicapped parking only and all others drivers have to hike in; (c) there are so many spots for handicapped parking that it seems disproportionate.

Handout 5.3b: Three Thought Experiments

Thought Experiment 1

Imagine that you are in a long line to use the restroom. There is one handicapped stall and eight regular stalls. All stalls are full. If a person in a wheelchair entered the line, would you let that person go ahead of you when the handicapped stall was free, if you were

The first in line?

The 10th in line?

The 20th in line?

Would any of your answers change if five people using wheelchairs entered the line?

Thought Experiment 2

You are waiting to board a Southwest Airlines flight. You have carry-on luggage you need to store in an overhead bin; if room runs out, you will have to check your bag. Also, you very much want an aisle or window (not a middle) seat. Preboarding is allowed for those with various disabilities and families with young children and those with service animals.

What number of people with disabilities (and their families) going ahead of you would it take before you felt it was unjust to you, if you were in boarding group A (the first group of about 30 people to board), group B (the next group of about 30 people to board), or group C (the last people to board the plane)?

Thought Experiment 3

You have applied for a job you very much want. The final decision is between you and a person who is blind. You are both equally qualified. Who do you think should get the job and why? Make your case for your decision.

Does the type of disability the other candidate has make a difference in your decision?

Activity 5.4: EYE SPY: Application of Laws

Activity: Take on tasks that a person with a disability might have to do. Each task involves some research and sometimes knowledge of rights and laws.

Where: At home, mostly on computer and phone and some outdoor areas in one's own neighborhood.

Purpose: Disability takes time and energy in ways that are mostly invisible to others. The purpose of this assignment is to show how important it is for people with disabilities to know their own rights, be nimble in figuring out how to get some things accomplished, and often pay extra for something that works for them.

Learning Objectives

1. Play EYE SPY (see Handout 5.4b), completing each task to the greatest degree possible.
2. Experience the extra time needed to accommodate one's own disability.
3. Select the appropriate laws and legal forms needed for specific tasks.
4. Analyze visibility of people with disabilities.
5. Assess your experience completing this assignment.

Materials: Handouts 5.4a/b (teacher copy and student copy), computer, and phone access.

Preparation: (A) It is helpful if students read a brief fact sheet on the Americans with Disabilities Act (ADA; https://adata.org/factsheet/ADA-overview). (B) If students have already been assigned a disability for the course, then they should use that disability for the relevant parts of this assignment (the two Y parts in the handouts). Otherwise, students should be assigned a disability. The discussion will be more interesting the week following this assignment if students are assigned different disabilities.

Time: 3 hours.

Possible Outcomes: There are many possible outcomes for each part of the assignment. Therefore, a teacher version of the handout showing possible issues that might arise is included.

Talking Points: See the teacher copy of Handout 5.4.

Grading Rubric: Suggest 2 points per letter (of EYE SPY) for a total of 12 points.

Handouts: 5.4a: Teacher Copy; 5.4b: Students Copy.

Additional Reading

Andrews, E. E., & Lund, E. M. (2015). Disability in psychology training: Where are we? *Training and Education in Professional Psychology*, *9*(3), 210–216.

Baumgartner, M. K., Dwertmann, D. J. G., Boehm, S. A., & Bruch, H. (2015). Job satisfaction of employees with disabilities: The role of perceived structural flexibility. *Human Resource Management*, *54*(2), 323–343. https://doi.org/10.1002/hrm.21673

Beatty, J. (2017). The complex nature of disability stigma in employment: Impact on access and opportunity. In S. B. Thomson & G. Grandy (Eds.), *Stigmas, work & organizations* (pp. 55–70). New York: Palgrave Macmillan.

Hasnain, R., & Balcazar, F. (2009). Predicting community- versus facility-based employment for transition-aged young adults with disabilities: The role of race, ethnicity, and support systems. *Journal of Vocational Rehabilitation*, *31*, 175–188. https://doi.org/10.3233/JVR-2009-0487

Sevak, P., Houtenville, A. J., Brucker, D. L., & O'Neill, J. (2015). Individual characteristics and the disability employment gap. *Journal of Disability Policy Studies*, *26*(2), 80–88. https://doi.org/10.1177/1044207315585823

Handout 5.4a: Teacher Copy

	Task	Possible Outcomes
E	Your place of employment doesn't have an automatic door opener at the entrance, which you need to enter the building without assistance. (a) Note who/what entity is responsible for making the accommodation. (b) Find the right agency to file a complaint in this regard. (c) Complete and attach the appropriate complaint form. (d) How easy or hard was this task?	Employment accommodation is covered by Title I (Employment) of the ADA. If the employer provides a service to the public, then it is also covered by Title II (Public Accommodations and Services). (a) The student's employer may not own the building, in which case human resources should contact the building owner or manager to request the accommodation. (b) The correct agency is the Equal Employment Opportunity Commission (EEOC). (c) Each state may have its own form, and there are different versions of the form; it is best to get it from the EEOC website.
Y	Make a list of probable workplace accommodations you would need for your assigned disability and your specific symptoms (list symptoms and the accommodations for those symptoms). *Do not use a generic list of accommodations from the Internet!*	It is very easy to go online and find a list of workplace accommodations. Some students simply cut and paste this list. However, they should think about their assigned disability specifically and have the list tailored to the needs of someone with that disability.
E	Go to a public place (e.g., coffee shop, restaurant, plaza) and count how many people with apparent disabilities you see in 30 minutes (e.g., those using a wheelchair, scooter, white cane, or service dog or using sign language). State your location and time of day. *Note: Therapy animals do not count; a service animal is likely to wear a vest stating "service" and is very unlikely to be carried.*	Some students forget to state their location. At least a few students will not see any apparently disabled people. Discussion can then be on the differences in locations across students, and whether/how some places are more "disability friendly" than others.

S	Go to a very busy parking lot and note the number of handicapped parking spaces and the approximate total number of parking spaces. Is at least one handicapped space available when you arrive? And 10 minutes later? Include your location and time of arrival.	Venues are likely to have some available spaces before 9 a.m., with fewer openings between 10 a.m. and 7 p.m. Medical facilities have more spaces than other venues. Was anyone parked illegally in a handicapped spot?
P	Find a place to modify your car so it can be driven with your *left* foot and the price. Note how easy or hard it was to find this information. (See picture included on student copy.)	This one can be very easy: go online and order a part from Amazon for about $150; find a van conversion service to install it. Or, it can be very difficult if the student starts on the wrong track: Calling a car dealership or service likely means the student will be told they do not do this, don't know who does, and that the student may have to buy a new car already altered (which is not the case).
Y	Find an article related to your assigned disability (or close to it) and workplace accommodations. Include the reference and abstract here. Then note what would be your takeaway from this article as a person with your assigned disability and your reaction to the article.	Some disabilities have fewer published articles, but there should be something on most disabilities or something close to the disability (e.g., if the student is assigned lupus but cannot find an article, there should be something on a different autoimmune disorder). More articles are in social work, occupational therapy, vocational rehabilitation, and organizational behavior than in psychology. The student should show evidence of having actually read the article!

Handout 5.4b: Student Copy

	Task	Outcome
E	Your place of employment doesn't have an automatic door opener at the entrance, which you need to enter the building without assistance. (a) Note who/what entity is responsible for making the accommodation. (b) Find the right agency to file a complaint. (c) Complete and attach the appropriate complaint form. (d) How easy or hard was this task?	
Y	Make a list of probable workplace accommodations you would need for your assigned disability and your specific symptoms (list symptoms and the accommodations for those symptoms). *Do not use a generic list of accommodations from the Internet!*	
E	Go to a public place (e.g., coffee shop, restaurant, plaza) and count how many people with apparent disabilities you see in 30 minutes (e.g., those using a wheelchair, scooter, white cane, or service dog or using sign language). State your location and time of day. *Note: Therapy animals do not count; a service animal is likely to wear a vest stating "service" and is very unlikely to be carried.*	
S	Go to a very busy parking lot and note the number of handicapped parking spaces and the approximate total number of parking spaces. Is at least one handicapped space available when you arrive? And 10 minutes later? Include your location and time of arrival.	

P	Find a place to modify your car so it can be driven with your *left* foot and the price. Note how easy or hard it was to find this information (see picture, below).  photo by Sara • copyright © 2006; all rights reserved	
Y	Find an article related to your assigned disability (or close to it) and workplace accommodations. Include the reference and abstract here. Then note what would be your takeaway from this article as a person with your assigned disability and your reaction to the article.	

6 Models of and Beliefs About Disability

HOW DISABILITY IS conceptualized is so fundamental to understanding of a person with disability and to culturally appropriate therapy that there are four activities in this section. They focus on the three main models of disability (moral, medical, and social). In Activity 6.1, students explore their illness beliefs as a first step to understanding models of disability. In Activity 6.2, students find media exemplars of the models. Only then is there an activity to help students explore their own model(s) of disability (Activity 6.3). In Activity 6.4, students apply the models to themselves and family members as if they themselves were newly diagnosed with a disability.

Teaching Disability. Rhoda Olkin, Oxford University Press. © Oxford University Press 2021.
DOI: 10.1093/oso/9780190850661.003.0006

Activity 6.1: Health, Illness, and Disability Beliefs

Activity: Answering questions about one's own beliefs about health, illness, and disability and comparing answers with a classmate or peer.

Where: In class.

Purpose: To uncover and explore one's belief system about health, illness, and disability.

Learning Objectives

1. Respond to specific questions about health, illness, and disability beliefs.
2. Describe the aspects that are coherent or contradictory.
3. Analyze responses to derive a belief system.
4. Compare one's belief system with that of a peer.

Materials: Handouts 6.1b: (Questions About Illness and Medication Beliefs) and 6.1c (Questions About Disability Beliefs).

Preparation: None required, but it is advisable that students read at least one article about pain beliefs before doing this activity (see Additional Reading). Explanation of the fear–avoidance pain model is advisable before students do this activity (see Handout 6.1a: For Instructors).

Time: *In class*: 1 hour total: 30 minutes for self-assessment, 20 minutes for comparison with a peer, and 10 minutes for group discussion. *As homework*: 1.5 hours total: 1 hour allowed to write answers to Handouts 6.1b and 6.1c, and 30 minutes to compare and contrast answers with a peer.

Possible Outcomes: Usually, we tend to view our own beliefs as the right ones and as similar to others' beliefs. Mostly these beliefs are subconscious and unarticulated. Some students may have more difficulty than others accessing their own beliefs. Also, it can be important to create safety in the discussion for those espousing various cultural beliefs that seem counter to current science (e.g., as noted in a Google search of the terms yin and yang: "Yin and yang are in constant flux. If one becomes unbalanced in the body, illness occurs. For example, since yin is cold, an excess of yin can cause illnesses such as insomnia and dry-mouth. Conversely, a yang deficiency can cause cold limbs and a sickly-complexion.").

Talking Points: Clinicians need to be able to talk to clients about their beliefs without sounding as if the client is responsible for the effects of those beliefs. Role playing this in class is helpful. For example, the Thompson and Woby (2017) article cited in Additional Reading suggests that clients need to achieve some "acceptance" of pain. How might this information be used with a client without criticizing or blaming or shaming the client? Discussion of the difference between "resignation" and "acceptance" is important, as the former leads to reduction of helpful behaviors and the latter leads to better tolerance of the chronic condition.

Grading Rubric: I suggest no grade if the exercise is done in class. If done outside class, there could be a written response to the questions on Handouts 6.1b and 6.1c (10 points) and a summary of the discussion and comparison of beliefs conducted with a peer (10 points).

Handouts: 6.1a: For Instructors; 6.1b: For Students—Questions About Illness and Medication Beliefs; 6.1c: For Students—Questions About Disability Beliefs.

Additional Reading

Arestedt, L., Benzein, E., & Persson, C. (2015). Families living with chronic illness: Beliefs about illness, family, and health care. *Journal of Family Nursing, 21*(2), 206–231.

Bell, J. M., & Wright, L. M. (2015). The illness beliefs model: Advancing practice knowledge about illness beliefs, family healing, and family interventions. *Journal of Family Nursing, 21*(2), 179–185.

Edmond, S. L., Enriquez, C. S., Millner, M. H., Nasri-Heir, C., & Heir, G. M. (2017). Is there an association between fear avoidance beliefs, and pain and disability in patients with orofacial pain? *Journal of Oral Rehabilitation, 44*(6), 426–433. https://doi.org/10.1111/joor.12503

Goering, S. (2015). Rethinking disability: The social model of disability and chronic disease. *Current Reviews in Musculoskeletal Medicine, 8*(2), 134–138.

Järemo, P., Arman, M., Gerdle, B., Larsson, B., & Gottberg, K. (2017). Illness beliefs among patients with chronic widespread pain: Associations with self-reported health status, anxiety and depressive symptoms and impact of pain. *BMC Psychology, 5*, 24–34.

Sato, N., Araki, A., Ito, R., & Ishigaki, K. (2015). Exploring the beliefs of Japanese mothers' care for a child with disabilities. *Journal of Family Nursing, 21*(2), 232–260.

Seng, E. K., Buse, D. C., Mayson, C., Klepper, J., Grosberg, B. M., Pavlovic, J. M., . . . Lipton, R. B. (2015). Migraine beliefs, psychiatric symptoms and migraine disability in a specialty headache clinic. *Headache, 55*, 178–179.

Thompson, D. P., & Woby, S. R. (2017). Acceptance in chronic neck pain: Associations with disability and fear avoidance beliefs. *Journal of Rehabilitation Research, 40*(3), 220–226.

Waddell, G., Newton, M., Henderson, I., Somerville, D., & Main, C. J. (1993). A Fear-Avoidance Beliefs Questionnaire (FABQ) and the role of fear-avoidance beliefs in chronic low back pain and disability. *Pain, 52*(2), 157–168. https://doi.org/10.1016/0304-3959(93)90127-B

Wisnivesky, J. P., Holguin, F., Busse, P. J., West, E., Goodman, E., Smith, V. L., . . . Federman, A. D. (2018). Differences in illness beliefs among obese and non-obese patients with asthma [Abstract]. *American Journal of Respiratory and Critical Care Medicine, 197*, A1088.

Handout 6.1a: For Instructors

The fear–avoidance model is hypothesized to be a key aspect of pain beliefs. Most studies support this model, though some studies do not find this model to explain the pain experience. The fear–avoidance model posits the following sequence:

> Pain → The personal experience of pain → Fear of pain→ Avoidance of activity (due to belief that it will increase pain) → Disuse, disability, depression → Increased experience of pain.

Handout 6.1b: For Students

Questions About Illness and Medication Beliefs

What illnesses did you have as a child?
What happened in your family when you were ill? How did everyone react?
Were there family remedies that were used (e.g., prayer, chicken soup, hot baths, cold compresses)?
Was it ever a fun thing to stay home from school sick? Did your parent(s) let you stay home? Did they send you to school anyway? What would they say about staying home/going to school?
Were there specific things your parent(s) did when you were sick (e.g., read to you, changed your sheets, fluffed your pillow, let you watch TV, gave you special foods)?
How quick were your parents to give you medications?
What were the beliefs about what caused the illnesses (e.g., viruses, stress, poor habits, a cold wind, tempting fate)?
Were the beliefs of your family consistent with your culture? Which were the same? Which were different?
Who in the family took medications regularly? What did they take? For what reasons? What were you told about this?
What are your beliefs about prescribed medications? Over-the-counter medications?
What are your beliefs about complementary medicine (e.g., acupuncture, massage, mindfulness, yoga)?
What does "wellness" mean to you?

Handout 6.1c: For Students

Questions About Disability Beliefs

1. Do you have any disabilities (as defined by the Americans with Disabilities Act)?
2. Did anyone in your immediate and your extended family have any disabilities?
3. What was the family's responses to disability?
4. Do you have religious or spiritual beliefs about disability?
5. Do you currently have close contact with a person with a disability (i.e., a partner, child, parent, sibling, close friend)?
6. What do you imagine to be the biggest problems facing most people with disabilities?
7. If you learned your child would have (a) moderate cerebral palsy, (b) Down syndrome, or (c) a heart defect requiring surgery shortly after birth, what would be your initial thoughts and reactions for each?
8. Did your reactions differ for questions 7a, 7b, and 7c?
9. You have one million dollars to spend; how would you divide it among these three things: (a) seeking means of preventing disabilities, (b) seeking cures for current disabling conditions, or (d) improving the lives of those currently living with disabilities?
10. How inclined would you be to date a person who (a) is blind; (b) uses a wheelchair; (c) has insulin-dependent diabetes; (d) has bipolar disorder; (e) has fibromyalgia?
11. Should people with disabilities get more, less, or the same government assistance as they do now?
12. Should there be financial incentives for businesses to hire people with disabilities?
13. Should there be affirmative action in employment for people with disabilities?
14. People with disability placards or license plates can park for free at parking meters; what are your thoughts about this?

Activity 6.2: Disability Belief Models in Real Life

Activity: Find examples of each model of disability (moral, medical, and social) in people, movies, newspapers, TV shows or news, magazines, or professional articles.

Where: Out and about, online, on TV, at home.

Purpose: To show that the models of disability are not only theoretical, but also occur in real life, and to make the concepts of models of disability more real.

Learning Objectives

1. Find examples of each of the models of disability (moral, medical, and social).
2. Critique the examples and explain how they fit one or more models.
3. Give samples of the language used in the examples found.
4. Analyze the sociocultural context of the examples found.

Materials: Readings.

Preparation: Students should read Olkin (1999, Chapter 2), World Health Organization (2001), and Handouts 6.2a and 6.2b. These should be discussed in class before assigning this activity. (Note that in Olkin, 1999, the social model is referred to as the "minority model," which is the same thing.) It is recommended that students do Activity 6.1 prior to Activity 6.2.

Time: Approximately 3 hours, not including preparation time in class.

Possible Outcomes: Students may have a hard time recognizing the models or not be able to find one of the models. The moral model may be less blatant but can be found in some movies. Most professional journals on health and medicine adhere to the medical model. Rehabilitation psychology is slowly moving toward the social model, but this model is more apparent in the *Disability & Society* journal and the *Journal of Disability Policy Studies*. Contrasting two articles, one in the journal *Health Psychology* and one in a disability journal, can be illuminating.

Talking Points: Students who already have one or more stigmatized or minority statuses tend to understand and relate to the idea of models more readily and have a more intuitive sense of the differences among them. "Pride"—gay pride, Black pride, disability pride—can be a good discussion topic. This can be done along with a discussion of language, specifically the way pride movements take back terms that historically have been used derogatorily and now are used within a group (e.g., dyke, bitch, or crip), and what happens when insiders versus outsiders use these terms.

Grading Rubric: 15 points for each example of a moral, a medical, or a social model or a mixed model, with (a) the explanation of how the sample exemplified one or more models, (b) samples of the language used, and (c) analysis of the sociocultural context (up to 45 points total).

Handouts: 6.2a: Comparison of Three Models of Disability; 6.2b: Language Associated with the Three Models of Disability; 6.2c: Instructions for Students, with an example.

Additional Reading

Beaudry, J. (2016). Beyond (models of) disability? *Journal of Medicine and Philosophy, 41*(2), 210–228.

Brown, S. E. (2003). Personal reflections on disability culture. *Review of Disability Studies, 1*(1), 1–9.

Darrow, A. (2013). Culturally responsive teaching: Understanding disability culture. *General Music Today, 26*(3), 32–34.

Dunn, D. S., & Andrews, E. E. (2015). Person-first and identity-first language: Developing psychologists' cultural competence using disability language. *American Psychologist, 70*(3), 255–264.

Dupre, M. (2012). Disability culture and cultural competence in social work. *Social Work Education, 31*(2), 168–183.

Ingstad, B., & Whyte, S. R. (Eds.). (1995). *Disability and culture.* Berkeley: University of California Press.

Jackson, M. A. (2018). Models of disability and human rights: Informing the improvement of built environment accessibility for people with disability at neighborhood scale? *Laws, 79*(1), 1–21. http://www.mdpi.com/2075-471X/7/1/10/htm or https://doi.org/10.3390/laws7010010

Llewellyn, A., & Hogan, K. (2000). The use and abuse of models of disability. *Disability & Society, 15*(1), 157–165.

Oliver, M. 2013. The social model of disability: Thirty years on. *Disability & Society, 28*(7), 1024–1026.

Olkin, R. (1999). Models of disability. In *What psychotherapists should know about disability* (Chapter 2). New York: Guilford Press.

Olkin, R. (2017). Disability-affirmative therapy III: Models of disability. In *Disability-affirmative therapy: A case formulation template for your clients with disabilities* (Chapter 6). New York: Oxford University Press.

Scotch, R. K. (2000). Models of disability and the Americans with Disabilities Act. *Berkeley Journal of Employment & Labor Law, 21*, 213–222.

United Nations. (2006). Convention on the Rights of Persons with Disabilities—Articles. https://www.un.org/development/desa/disabilities/convention-on-the-rights-of-persons-with-disabilities/convention-on-the-rights-of-persons-with-disabilities-2.html

World Health Organization. (2001). Towards a common language for functioning, disability and health. International Classification of Functioning, Disability and Health (ICF). http://www.who.int/classifications/icf/en/

Handout 6.2a: Comparison of Three Models of Disability

	Moral	Medical	Social
Meaning of disability	Disability is a manifestation of poor moral character, sins, evil, lack of faith. Conversely, it is a test of faith or given selectively to someone who can withstand it.	A defect in or failure of a bodily system or impairment in a body function. It is inherently abnormal.	Disability is a social construct. Problems arise from the mismatch between the person's abilities/needs and the environment, and in the attitudes of others.
Moral implications	The disability brings shame to the person with the disability and his/her family. It affects marriageability and future vocational prospects and independence.	Something has gone wrong or is damaged due to genetics, bad health habits, medical procedure, person's behavior, accident.	Disability is a normal part of the human spectrum of differences. Society has failed a segment of its citizens and oppresses them.
Sample ideas	"God gives us only that which we can bear" or "It is my fate or karma" or "It is my burden to bear."	Clinical descriptions of "patients" in medical terminology. Isolation of body parts or system functions.	"Nothing about us without us." "Civil rights, not charity."
Origins	Oldest model. Most prevalent worldwide. Is prevalent in specific cultures within the United States	Mid–nineteenth century during the Enlightenment. Most common model in the United States. Predominant model in psychology, many rehabilitation clinics, and journals.	Early 1900s, then dormant until about mid-1970s: First televised demonstrations by people with disabilities; beginning of disability activism.
Goals of intervention	Spiritual or divine, acceptance, forbearance.	"Cure" or amelioration of the disability to the greatest extent possible.	Political, economic, social, and policy systems, increased access & inclusion.

Handout 6.2b: Language Associated with the Three Models of Disability

Model	Language Example: Descriptive	Comments
Moral	Joe, who has been wheelchair bound since he was afflicted with multiple sclerosis (MS), can only feed himself dinner by using special utensils.	Note the use of emotionally laden words such as *wheelchair bound, afflicted, can only, special.* Joe's differences not only are emphasized but also have a negative value placed on those differences.
Medical	Joe, a patient who uses a wheelchair as a result of partial paraplegia due to MS, eats dinner using utensils that compensate for reduced grip.	Joe is described using precise medical terms and diagnosis such as partial paraplegia and MS. Note, also, the idea of compensation for a failed bodily function (reduced grip).
Social	Joe, a man with MS who uses a chair, eats dinner.	In this description Joe's action of eating dinner is more salient; people-first language is used (a man with MS); some shorthand from the disability community is used (a chair denotes a wheelchair); and there is omission of irrelevant disability factors (special utensils). Capability is more pronounced, rather than failure or inability.
	Language Example: Clinical	
Moral	My son can't walk straight; he can't use his right hand well, so he can't cut his own food. We have to do many things for him; it's very hard.	The focus here is exclusively on problems, on what cannot be done, and how this negatively affects his relationships in the family (burden).

Medical	My son has right hemiplegia but his brain works okay.[a] He's learning to be more independent.	The description is very medical. The words *cerebral palsy* [CP] are avoided as they carry negative stigma. The parent is quick to assure that it isn't a more stigmatized disability ("his brain works okay"), and that the goal is increased independence (a very mainstream American value). (Note that hemiplegia implies some brain damage.)
Social	My son has CP. We want to know how to help him make more friends and to be happy.	The diagnosis is given without concern for the connotations. The focus is on quality of life (friends, happiness) and how the parents can help the son, not on what a burden he is.
	Language Example: Positives	
Moral	"I stepped on a land mine when I was 12. Now every day I wake up in pain, and it reminds me to thank Allah that I am alive."	Where we might have expected this person to say "and it reminds me to curse the land mines," we instead hear a positive meaning ascribed to the pain.
Medical	"Everyone has something to cope with. There are incredible advances all the time, and I know I can cope with this."	Disability is seen as no different from the "burdens" others might have. There is hope and belief in a better future—cure or amelioration of the condition—and a belief in personal strength.
Social	"I got to go to summer camp, where all the kids had disabilities. It was great, the best thing. Disability was just normal, no big deal."	The person feels a sense of belonging and a place in which disability not only is a unifier, but also is relegated to the background for once.

	Language Example: Negatives	
Moral	"It is my wife's fault that our son has this disorder. She had too much stress during pregnancy."	There is blame and ascription of a cause of the disability that lies with one person (the mother) and causes negative feelings toward that person.
Medical	"Doctors don't know anything; they can't help me; they just want to pass me around as a specimen."	There is hopelessness, a lack of collaboration with the medical professionals, and distrust of motives.
Social	"It will never change; people with disabilities will always be at the bottom of the totem pole. I can't change the world; that's just the way it is."	There is hopelessness, this time at the enormity of tasks to be undertaken, and the belief that some group (those with disabilities) will always be at the bottom of the social pecking order because that is human nature.

Handout 6.2c: Instructions for Students

Find examples of each model of disability (moral, medical, and social) in real life. You may use movies, documentaries, newspapers, TV shows or news, popular personalities, magazines, or professional articles (or other, with teacher permission). For each example,

a. Give as much information about the example as you can or include it verbatim.
b. Critique the example and explain how it fits one or more of the three models.
c. Give samples of the language used in each example found.
d. Analyze the sociocultural context of the example.

EXAMPLE

a. The character of Artie Abrams on the TV show *Glee* uses a wheelchair and is one of two regular characters with a visible disability on the show (the other is Becky Jackson, a woman with Down syndrome, played by Lauren Potter, a woman with Down syndrome). However, the actor playing the character in a wheelchair, Kevin McHale, is able-bodied. In one episode, there is a dream sequence where Artie gets out of his wheelchair and dances. The initial desire by another character to help Artie walk, and by Artie himself, represents the medical model, in that "cure" or "normalcy" is the goal. However, Artie comes to reject this model, asserting that he must be accepted as is, a person in a wheelchair. This is a move toward the social model of disability, that is, self-acceptance and some nascent disability pride.
b. This example shows a variety of viewpoints and conveys some complex ideas. It tackles the desire of others to see people with disabilities be "normalized." Then it veers toward self-acceptance (by Artie) and rejection of others (his potential girlfriend) who cannot accept him as is. But by hiring an able-bodied actor to play this role, the director and/or producers are conveying a different message—actors with disabilities could not be found or were not right for this role. When using the wheelchair, Artie makes subtle movements that are more akin to those of an able-bodied than a paraplegic person, making the wheelchair more of a prop than an appendage of Artie.
c. The following bits of dialogue show not only that Artie is able to joke about his wheelchair, but also that he acknowledges that it makes things harder for him and that others may have distorted or incorrect views about him.

- In response to interviewer saying, "I heard you were sitting with Cheerios in the lunchroom": Artie responds, "I'm usually seen sitting."
- In response to another student saying, "I thought you were a senior": Artie responds, "Optical illusion, the chair adds a year."
- To potential girlfriend: Artie responds, "I want to be very clear; I still have the use of my penis."
- In response to hearing a bad singer: Artie responds, "Her ears should get to park in my handicapped spot."
- When the Glee instructor says, "How much harder Artie has to work just to keep up." Artie responds, "Preach."

d. Artie is a White heterosexual male (so there is no intersectionality of minority statuses) in high school, a contradictory time of both conformity and desire to be unique. He belongs to the putatively "out-group" of kids in Glee, but within that group there is great diversity. Still, he is odd man out in several scenes (jumping on mattresses for a commercial or needing a wheelchair-accessible bus), and he is the only one of the group who costs the school money (e.g., for the accessible bus).

Activity 6.3: Assessing Models of Disability

Activity: Assessing the model(s) of disability (i.e., the belief systems) of peers.

Where: All parts can be done either inside or outside class (see Time).

Purpose: To begin putting different beliefs about health, illness, and disability into an explanatory scheme.

Learning Objectives

1. Interview a peer in the class about his/her/their beliefs about health, illness, and disability. You can use the questions in Handout 6.1a.
2. Together fill in Handout 6.3b with the degree of positives and negatives of each model to which the peer ascribes.
3. Reverse roles and repeat 1 and 2.
4. Compare results with your peer.
5. Assess your learning.

Materials: None.

Preparation: This activity cannot be done without some groundwork. It is highly recommended that students first do Activity 6.1 (Health, Illness, and Disability beliefs) and Activity 6.2 (Disability Belief Models in Real Life). These three activities in sequence will explicate the models of disability and make them more tangible and this activity more doable.

Time: 2 hours total: (A) 45 minutes for peer interview and recording of data on the three models, 45 minutes to switch roles; (B) 15 minutes to compare responses with peer; and (C) 15 minutes to assess and write what has been learned.

Possible Outcomes: Students may be tempted to assess themselves, but I have found that they have trouble determining their own models, and it is easier to do the assessment on someone else. This activity can unearth beliefs and values that students absorbed early in life that they are now uncomfortable with and hence experience some cognitive dissonance. The portrait that emerges is of beliefs as they are right now rather than beliefs as we wish them to be. It can be good to remind them that this is exactly what happens for clients.

Talking Points: Our beliefs in models come from a variety of sources, with family and religion being the most dominant sources. Other sources include race/ethnicity, media, personal acquaintances, peers, geographical area, and community. It is good to explore in class (a) what surprised students, (b) where they think their beliefs originated, (c) how diverse beliefs were across the classroom, and (d) what aspects of their beliefs they would wish to change (if any).

Grading Rubric: 10 points total: 5 points for peer interview and recording of data, 5 points for the comparison with peer and assessment of what has been learned.

Handouts: 6.3a: Instructions for Students; 6.3b: Exploring Models.

Additional Reading

Corraliza, J. A., & Berenguer, J. (2000). Environmental values, beliefs and actions. *Environment and Behavior, 32*(6), 832–848.

Daudji, A., Eby, S., Foo, T., Ladak, F., Sinclair, C., Landry, M. D., . . . Gibson, B. E. (2010). Perceptions of disability among South Asian immigrant mothers of children with disabilities in Canada: Implications for rehabilitation service delivery. *Disability & Rehabilitation, 33*(6), 511–521. https://doi.org/10.3109/09638288.2010.498549

Fisher, K. R., & Purcal, C. (2017). Policies to change attitudes toward people with disabilities. *Scandinavian Journal of Disability Research, 19*(2), 161–174. https://doi.org/10.1080/15017419.2016.1222303

King, G., Desmarais, C., Lindsay, S., Pierart, G., & Tetrault, S. (2014). The roles of effective communication and client engagement in delivering culturally sensitive care to immigrant parents of children with disabilities. *Disability & Rehabilitation, 37*(15), 1372–1381.

Lawton, K. E., Gerdes, A. C., Haack, L. M., & Schneider, B. (2014). Acculturation, cultural values, and Latino parental beliefs about the etiology of ADHD. *Administration and Policy in Mental Health and Mental Health Services Research, 41*(2), 189–204.

Lindsay, S., Tetrault, S., Desmaris, C., King, G., & Pierart, G. (2014). Social workers as "cultural brokers" in providing culturally sensitive care to immigrant families raising a child with a physical disability. *Health & Social Work, 39*(2), e10–e20. https://doi.org/10.1093/hsw/hlu009

Lu, J., Webber, W., Romero, D., & Chirino, C. (2017). Changing attitudes toward people with disabilities using public media: An experimental study. *Rehabilitation Counseling Bulletin, 61*(3), 175–186.

Suggs, D. W., & Guthrie, J. L. (2017). Disabling prejudice: A case study of images of Paralympic athletes and attitudes toward people with disabilities. *International Journal of Sport Communication, 10*(2), 258–276.

Walker, R. C., Howard, K., Morton, R. L., Palmer, S. C., Marshall, M. R., & Tong, A. (2016). Patient and caregiver values, beliefs and experiences when considering home dialysis as a treatment option—A semi-structured interview study. *Nephrology Dialysis Transplantation, 31*(1), 133–141. https://doi.org/10.1093/ndt/gfv330

Handout 6.3a: Instructions for Students

You will pair up with a peer from class. For approximately 45 minutes, one of you will interview the other about beliefs and values related to health, illness, and disability. The goal of the interview is to be able to fill out the figure in Handout 6.3b.

1. Interview a peer in the class about his/her/their beliefs about health, illness, and disability. Use Handouts 6.1a, 6.1b, and 6.3b as an interview guide of areas to cover.
2. Together fill in Handout 6.3b with the degree of positives and negatives of each model to which the peer ascribes. Write in words next to each area. For example, if the person believes illness comes from imbalance, write "imbalance" in the moral model, either in the positive portion (if this belief helps the person) or the negative portion (if this belief causes shame or guilt).
3. Reverse roles and repeat Steps 1 and 2.
4. Compare results with your peer. Where are they the same or different? How might your beliefs reflect your gender, age, socioeconomic background, race/ethnicity, religion, sexual orientation, disability status, country of origin?
5. Assess your learning and write ½ to 1 page about what you have learned.

Handout 6.3b: Exploring Models

On the next pages you will see three models of disability. *Models* describe how people view disability. There is no right or wrong model, and many people believe in elements of all three models. Please rate how much you agree with the models that follow.

Model A

- A disability is an abnormality in the body or brain of an individual.
- Medical and technological advances have improved the lives of those individuals with disabilities.
- Research about disabilities should mainly focus on two things:
  1. Prevention—keeping others from developing a disability.
  2. Cure—helping those who already have a disability remove it.
- Treatment of a disability should mainly focus on two things:
  1. Helping the person with the disability adjust to their environment as much as possible.
  2. Removing the disability from the person as much as possible.
- People with disabilities are patients who receive help from trained professionals such as doctors.

Please rate how much you agree with the above model.

Not at all ○	○	○	○	○	○	○	○	○	○ Completely
0	1	2	3	4	5	6	7	8	9

Model B

- Due to the process of enduring a disability, the person with the disability and their family members can grow from the experience in the mental, spiritual, and/or emotional spheres.
- Individuals with disabilities and their family members are chosen to endure the disability as a test of faith.
- The presence of a disability brings shame to the person with the disability and their family members.
- Disability may result as a punishment for that person's or their family's wrongdoings.

- Although a disability may impair a person in one area of their life, it can lead to a superior ability level in other areas of their life. For example, some cultures believe that individuals with epilepsy have a special connection to God when they have their seizures.
- Enduring disability brings you closer to your spirituality or God.

Please rate how much you agree with the above model.

Not at all ○	○	○	○	○	○	○	○	○	○ Completely

MODEL C

- People with disabilities are members of a minority group—that is, persons with disabilities—similar to people from an ethnic minority group. They feel kinship and belonging with other persons with disabilities.
- People with disabilities may receive negative treatment (e.g., prejudice, discrimination, and limited access to resources) because they have a disability.
- Research and policy about disabilities should concentrate on improving the environment so that it is more accessible and accommodating for persons with disabilities.
- The best way to improve the lives of people with disabilities is through strong enforcement of laws (e.g., Americans with Disabilities Act) and equal opportunity.
- Public education is needed to combat stigma and discrimination against disability.

Please rate how much you agree with the above model.

Not at all ○	○	○	○	○	○	○	○	○	○ Completely
0	1	2	3	4	5	6	7	8	9

Handout 6.3c: Assessing the model(s) of disability

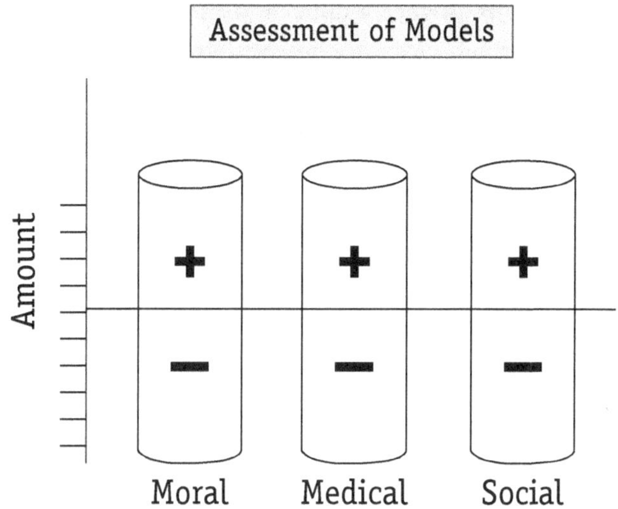

Activity 6.4: You Are Newly Diagnosed

Activity: Each student is assigned a different diagnosis, one acquired after birth. They will research their new diagnosis, potential symptoms, probable course, possible medications and treatments, gender and cultural factors, then make decisions about their immediate future. These will be shared and discussed in class.

Where: At home on a computer, then posted for peers, then discussed in class.

Purpose: To be able to better understand and help clients who are more recently diagnosed.

Learning Objectives

1. To utilize skills in Internet research to find reliable information about a specific diagnosis.
2. To experience having to make choices of medications, treatments, and lifestyle options when newly diagnosed.
3. To clearly articulate to peers the main symptoms, treatments, and other factors related to the diagnosis.
4. To explore the differences across diagnoses assigned to classmates.

Materials: Bowl with diagnoses to be randomly picked by each student in class. The list should include conditions that are acquired after birth so that a student could be newly diagnosed with the disorder (see Handout 6.4a for a list of possible diagnoses).

Preparation: A list of possible diagnoses to be chosen by students. If the class is large, the same diagnosis can be given to more than one student, and those students can then work together.

Time: 20 minutes in class to go over requirements for the assignment. Allow students 1 month to do the assignment at home and post it, then 1 week for students to read each other's work. One class period to compare and discuss findings.

Possible Outcomes: Many diagnoses are more prevalent among women (e.g., autoimmune disorders), and a few are more prevalent in men (e.g., spinal cord injury). There are ethnic differences in rates of many disorders, and some are related to specific ethnic groups (e.g., sickle cell disease).

Talking Points: Some diagnoses are quite common (e.g., arthritis, type 2 diabetes), and others are rarer (ankylosing spondylitis). Some affect expected life span (e.g., amyotrophic lateral sclerosis), and others are unlikely to do so (e.g., amputation; relapsing and remitting type MS).The effects of the diagnoses on activities of daily living are extremely varied, and some disorders progress while others do not. Some are highly visible, and others can be concealed. As students discuss the diagnoses, it is important to note these differences. In addition, the degree of stigma varies; why is that, and what determines the level of stigma?

Grading Rubric: 10 points for Question 1 on Handout 6.4b; 8 points for the remaining questions, 2 points for clarity of presentation (or for creativity).

Handouts: 6.4a: Possible diagnoses; 6.4b: Instructions for Students.

Additional Reading

Baldridge, D. C., & Kulkarni, M. (2017). The shaping of sustainable careers post hearing loss: Toward greater understanding of adult onset disability, disability identity, and career transitions. *Human Relations*, *70*(10), 1217–1236. https://doi.org/10.1177/0018726716687388

Choi, S. (2018). Midlife adults with functional limitations: Comparison of adults with early- and late-onset arthritis-related disability. *Disability and Health Journal*, *11*(3), 374–381. https://doi.org/10.1016/j.dhjo.2017.12.006

Hersh, M. (2015). Cane use and late onset visual impairment. *Technology and Disability*, *27*(3), 103–116.

Hilberink, S. R., van der Slot, W. M. A., & Klem, M. (2017). Health and participation problems in older adults with long-term disability. *Disability and Health Journal*, *10*(2), 361–366. https://doi.org/10.1016/j.dhjo.2016.12.004

Shi, Y. Z., Xiang, Y. T., Yang, Y., Zhang, N., Wang, S., Ungvari, G. S., . . . Wang, C. X. (2017). Depression after minor stroke: The association with disability and quality of life—A 1-year follow-up study. *Geriatric Psychiatry*, *31*(4), 421–427. https://doi.org/10.1002/gps.4353

Tsuruoka, Y., Takahashi, M., Suzuki, M., Sato, K., & Shirayama, Y. (2016). Utility of the Neurobehavioral Cognitive Status Examination (COGNISTAT) in differentiating between depressive states in late-life depression and late-onset Alzheimer's disease: A preliminary study. *Annals of General Psychiatry*, *15*(3), 1–8. https://doi.org/10.1186/s12991-016-0091-5

Handout 6.4a: Possible Diagnoses

Amputation of dominant hand from explosive device
Amyotrophic lateral sclerosis
Ankylosing spondylitis
Atherosclerosis
Cardiovascular disease
Chronic inflammatory demyelinating polyneuropathy
Chronic obstructive pulmonary disease
Crohn's disease
Diabetes—type II
Fibromyalgia
Huntington disease
Lupus
Macular degeneration
Ménière disease
Moderately severe hearing loss
Multiple sclerosis—relapsing and remitting type
Multiple sclerosis—secondary progressive type
Parkinson disease
Psoriatic arthritis
Rheumatoid arthritis
Schizophrenia
Spinal cord injury—T10
Spinal cord injury—L2
Tourette syndrome
Traumatic brain injury from car accident

Handout 6.4b: Instructions for Students

Regarding your diagnosis, consider the following:

1. Just what is it: What are the primary symptoms, and will the symptoms progress? Does the diagnosis affect your expected life span? What does your diagnosis mean for your activities of daily living and functioning? Are the symptoms visible to others? Will you need assistive equipment or technology? What might have caused the disorder? Do you experience pain? Fatigue? Weakness? Falling?
2. Is there a national organization devoted to your diagnosis?
3. What is available online about your diagnosis from various sources (e.g., the national organization, Wikipedia, Mayo Clinic, WebMD, chat rooms, online forums, and newsletters)?
4. Are there decisions you need to make about medications for your diagnosis?
5. Will you disclose your new diagnosis and, if so, to whom?
6. What might be the reactions of various people (e.g., parents, siblings, partners, friends) to your new diagnosis?
7. What accommodations might you need in school or work?
8. How might this diagnosis affect your decision to have children? To get pregnant? How to parent?
9. What is your intersectionality—What other characteristics do you possess, and how do these interact with your new diagnosis?

7 Everyday Issues

THE THREE ACTIVITIES in this section explore some hidden aspects of disability. The financial and time costs are illustrated in Activity 7.1. In Activity 7.2, pain—one of the most frequent sequelae of disability—is explored experientially. In Activity 7.3, the media messages about disability are probed because such messages will have particular resonance for your clients with disabilities.

Teaching Disability. Rhoda Olkin, Oxford University Press. © Oxford University Press 2021.
DOI: 10.1093/oso/9780190850661.003.0007

Activity 7.1: The Time and Financial Costs of Disability

Activity: Online research to find the costs of various disability assistive devices or modified equipment.

Where: On computer and phone.

Purpose: Economic status is a key variable for those with disabilities, in that disability costs money. Some problems related to accessibility can be solved with money. However, many modifications or types of equipment are not covered by insurance (either private or government). The purpose of this activity is to go through some research, cost analyses, and decision-making processes required for various devices or modifications and to show some of the hidden costs of disability.

Learning Objectives

1. Research specific items to find the highest and lowest prices.
2. Select which item you would choose, balancing cost and quality.
3. Compile prices for individual items and for total expenditures.
4. Assess your own learning in this activity.

Materials: Handouts 7.1a: Instructions for Teachers and 7.1b: Instructions for Students.

Preparation: None.

Time: 2 to 5 hours.

Possible Outcomes: Some general principles cut across most items: (a) Items are more expensive in medical supply stores than in hardware or general stores. (b) Walmart is generally the least expensive, but quality, warranty, and dependability may be of a lesser degree. (c) There is a vast range of prices, and some prices are outrageous. (d) It is extremely helpful if there is a family member who is handy (e.g., to install a grab bar; to install the left foot driver), so that you don't have to hire someone to do installation. (e) It is difficult to find some items, and if an item is scarce or available only in one model, then choice is narrowed (e.g., the crib without a foot mechanism may only be available in high-end cribs, priced at a premium). For the hand controls on a car, if this is a new modification, the person may be required to get an evaluation by an occupational therapist and/or a prescription for the modification, then take a class on driving with hand controls. The teletypewriter (TTY) is available for free from the phone company for businesses with a demonstrated need (e.g., those that provide a public service). The irony is that it is difficult to demonstrate the need until there is at least one deaf or hard-of-hearing caller or client, but there won't be a deaf or hard-of-hearing caller or client until there is a mechanism for communicating with the business.

Talking Points: There are great income inequalities between people with and without disabilities. In addition, people with disabilities experience conversion disadvantage, that is, the inability to turn income into goods or activities due to paying out of pocket for many items, accommodations, assistive devices, or personal assistance. Many, if not most, of the costs of disability are hidden to others. The activity highlights some of the time and financial costs of disability. Some students may be frustrated with the searches, but items were selected that were real needs (i.e., not esoteric ones). Some items have workarounds; for example, a bassinet could be substituted for a crib for about the first 4 months of life, then a modification could be made to a crib that uses a foot pedal so that it could be pushed by hand. Adapted baby care equipment does exist, but can be hard to find and expensive as it generally is not a mass-produced product. (The Tuleja and DeMoss (1999) article referenced in Additional Reading was one of the first professional articles on the topic.)

Grading Rubric: 2 points for the highest and lowest price for each of the seven items (14 points); 2 points total for selecting each item; 1 point for compiling total cost of all items; and 3 points for assessment of own learning. (20 points total)

Handouts: 7.1a: Instructions for Teachers; 7.1b: Instructions for Students.

Additional Reading

Carlson, T. (2014). 10 amazing products for parents with disabilities. https://blog.themobilityresource.com/blog/post/10-amazing-products-for-parents-with-disabilities

Charters, E., Gillett, L., & Simpson, G. K. (2014). Efficacy of electronic portable assistive devices for people with acquired brain injury: A systematic review. *Neuropsychological Rehabilitation, 25*(1), 82–121. https://doi.org/10.1080/09602011.2014.942672

Freedman, V. A., Kasper, J. D., & Spillman, B. C. (2016). Successful aging through successful accommodation with assistive devices. *Journals of Gerontology, Series B, 72*(2), 300–309. https://doi.org/10.1093/geronb/gbw102

Jutai, J., & Day, H. (2002). Psychosocial Impact of Assistive Devices Scale. *Technology & Disability, 14*(3), 107–111.

Martins, A. C., Pinheiro, J., Farias, B., & Jutai, J. (2016). Psychosocial impact of assistive technologies for mobility and their implications for active ageing. *Technologies, 4*(3), 28–37. https://doi.org/10.3390/technologies4030028

Mithin, J., Aitken, Z., Ziersch, A., & Kavanagh, A. M. (2015). Inequality in social capital and health between people with and without disabilities. *Social Science & Medicine, 126*, 26–35. https://doi.org/10.1016/j.socscimed.2014.12.009

Orellano-Colón, E. M., Jutai, J., Santiago, A., Torres, V., Benítez, K., & Torres, M. (2016). Assistive technology needs and measurement of the psychosocial impact of assistive technologies for independent living of older Hispanics: Lessons learned. *Technologies, 4*(3), 21–33. https://doi.org/10.3390/technologies4030021

Pazzaglia, M., & Molinari, M. (2016). The embodiment of assistive devices—From wheelchair to exoskeleton. *Physics of Life Reviews, 16*, 163–175. https://doi.org/10.1016/j.plrev.2015.11.006

Tuleja, C., & DeMoss, A. (1999). Babycare assistive technology. *Technology & Disability, 11*(1–2), 71–78.

Handout 7.1a: Instructions for Teachers

Directions for this activity are on the student copy, but there are additional options you might consider:

1. Give a prize to the person whose total for all items was the lowest and to the person whose total was the highest (e.g., a $5 gift card).
2. Allot five bonus points if a student calls an insurance company to find out which of the seven items would be covered, either wholly or in part, under insurance.

Handout 7.1b: Instructions for Students

Instructions

Below are listed some common disability accommodations and devices.

- Your first goal is to find the least and most expensive versions of these items that you can. You must "buy" the items new (i.e., no used versions). Descriptions of the items are included so that everyone is looking for the same type of item.
- Second, decide if you would want the least expensive version or, if not, which version you would want for yourself and why.
- Third, add up the total costs of all the items you chose.
- Fourth, write a one-page summary of your experience of completing the assignment and what you learned from this activity.

Items

1. A 36-inch grab bar to screw into the wall, plus installation.
2. Matching shoes to buy, with one foot a size 7 (adult) and the other foot a size 5 (large child or small adult).
3. A manual wheelchair: not a push chair, but one you propel yourself. Two large back wheels with rims to propel, two small front wheels; footrest.
4. An electric wheelchair with two large wheels in the middle, smaller wheels in back and smaller wheels in front; footrest and headrest; tiller control. The back of the chair should be able to recline. (Make sure the wheelchair works for someone who is your height.)
5. A TTY (teletypewriter phone, also called a TDD, or telecommunications device for the deaf) for your "business" (imagine that you are a psychotherapist in a group practice).
6. A place to do a car alteration that allows you to drive a regular car but with hand controls only.
7. A crib that has a side that opens by using only your hands (instead of your foot to unlatch the release).

Activity 7.2: The Pain Experience

Activity: Having students experience mild discomfort for about a half hour, using different methods of describing pain and ways of coping with pain. The discomfort is induced by wearing a clothespin on the earlobe for 30 minutes. About 1 hour later, after clothespins have been removed from ears, students are asked about reactions to being asked to put the clothespins back on their ears (which they will not actually do).

Where: In class.

Purpose: To understand how different ways of describing pain work for different people; to experience coping with pain; to illustrate fear of pain.

Learning Objectives

1. Experience mild discomfort.
2. Utilize four methods of describing pain.
3. Identify various coping mechanisms.
4. Assess effects of the fear of pain.
5. Describe pain beliefs.

Materials: Clothespins.

Preparation: Bring clothespins to class, one per student (and one for instructor, if instructor participates, which is recommended).

Time: 30 minutes to experience clothespin on ear and to utilize pain description methods; 20 minutes to discuss coping mechanisms and learning from activity.

Possible Outcomes: A pain that is fairly mild grows more irritating with time. Some students may elect to remove the clothespin early (which is fine). Those with preexisting pain may find this activity harder (to undergo additional pain) or easier (in comparison to more severe pain).

Talking Points: How students think about pain and what they say to themselves about the clothespin and the experience will greatly affect their emotional responses. It is helpful to first have them name their emotional reactions, then try to uncover the thoughts they had during the experience. Notice the different reactions across students and inquire about what might account for these differences. Ask them to imagine that you were going to tell them to put the clothespin on for another 30 minutes: What reactions do they have to this idea? What does this tell them about people who live with chronic or intermittent pain?

Grading Rubric: No grade.

Handouts: 7.2a: Instructions for Teachers; 7.2b: Instructions for Students (with several pain scales).

Additional Reading

Ehde, D. M., Jensen, M. P., Engel, J. M., Turner, J. A., Hoffman, A. J., & Cardenas, D. D. (2003). Chronic pain secondary to disability: A review. *Clinical Journal of Pain, 19*, 3–17.

Fish, R. A., McGuire, B., Hogan, M., Morrison, T. G., & Stewart, I. (2010). Validation of the chronic pain acceptance questionnaire (CPAQ) in an Internet sample and development and preliminary validation of the CPAQ-8. *Pain, 149*, 435–443. https://doi.org/10.1016/j.pain.2009.12.016

Jensen, M. P., Moore, M. R., Bockow, T. B., Ehde, D. M., & Engel, J. M. (2011). Psychosocial factors and adjustment to chronic pain in persons with physical disabilities: A systematic review. *Archives of Physical Medicine & Rehabilitation, 92*, 146–160. https://doi.org/10.1016/j.apmr.2010.09.021

Kranz, D., Bollinger, A., & Nilges, P. (2010). Chronic pain acceptance and affective well-being: A coping perspective. *European Journal of Pain (London, England), 14*, 1021–1025. https://doi.org/10.1016/j.ejpain.2010.03.010

Kratz, A. L., Hirsh, A. T., Ehde, D. M., & Jensen, M. P. (2013). Acceptance of pain in neurological disorders: Associations with functioning and psychological well-being. *Rehabilitation Psychology, 58*(1), 1–9.

McCracken, L. M. (2010). Toward understanding acceptance and psychological flexibility in chronic pain. *Pain, 149*, 420–421. https://doi.org/:10.1016/j.pain.2010.02.036

McCracken, L. M., & Eccleston, C. (2003). Coping or acceptance: What to do about chronic pain? *Pain, 105*, 197–204.

Viane, I., Crombez, G., Eccleston, C., Devulder, J., & De Corte, W. (2004). Acceptance of the unpleasant reality of chronic pain: Effects upon attention to pain and engagement with daily activities. *Pain, 112*, 282–288. https://doi.org/10.1016/j.pain.2004.09.008

Von Korff, M., Ormel, J., Keefe, F. J., & Dworkin, S. F. (1992). Grading the severity of chronic pain. *Pain, 50*, 133–149.

Vowles, K. E., & McCracken, L. M. (2008). Acceptance and values-based action in chronic pain: A study of treatment effectiveness and process. *Journal of Consulting and Clinical Psychology, 76*, 397–407. https://doi.org/10.1037/0022-006X.76.3.397

Vowles, K. E., McCracken, L. M., McLeod, C., & Eccleston, C. (2008). The Chronic Pain Acceptance Questionnaire: Confirmatory factor analysis and identification of patient subgroups. *Pain, 140*, 284–291. https://doi.org/10.1016/j.pain.2008.08.012

Wiech, K. (2016). Deconstructing the sensation of pain: The influence of cognitive processes on pain perception. *Science, 354*(6312), 584–587.

Handout 7.2a: Instructions for Teachers

Part A: Give each student a clothespin and ask them to put the clothespin on their earlobe. (If a student cannot do this for any reason, another location is the skin fold between thumb and forefinger.) Tell students that they will be asked to keep the clothespin on for 30 minutes, and show them the time on the clock, so they can track the time remaining before they can remove the clothespin. During the first 20 minutes go about other business of the class. For the last 10 minutes have students use the four methods of describing the pain they are currently experiencing.

Part B: Ask students to discuss the four methods of describing pain, and the methods of coping they used for the 30 minutes.

Part C: At least 30 minutes after doing the experience with the clothespin, tell students that they will be repeating the experience with the clothespins (which in fact they will not be doing). Ask them their reactions to the prospect of re-placing the clothespins on themselves—this is about the fear of pain, and what people do in reaction to the prospect of pain. End by assuring them they will not be doing the experience of the clothespins again. Collect clothespins.

Handout 7.2b: Instructions for Students

Pain can be difficult to describe to another person. Pain is subjective, and there are many ways to describe pain. Below are several methods of describing your pain to another person. Using these different methods will help you understand your experience better. Please feel free to make changes or notes on each of the scales if it helps to better describe your pain.

You may be experiencing more than one site or type of pain. For some questions, you will be asked to respond to the pain that is due to the clothespin experience. For other questions, you will be asked to describe *all* of the pain you may be experiencing.

A. *Using a pain scale to describe pain intensity*: For this question please consider *all* of the pain you are experiencing right now.
   0 = No pain
   1 = Very mild, almost unnoticeable pain
   3 = Mild but noticeable pain, such as the beginning of a headache
   5 = Moderate and very noticeable pain, such as a throbbing headache
   7 = Considerable pain that takes your attention, such as a migraine
   9 = Almost unbearable pain that commands all of your attention
   10 = The most pain you can imagine or have ever experienced
B. *Using words to describe the type of pain you are experiencing*: For this question please describe the pain due to the clothespin. Check all that apply.

_____ Achy	_____ Electric	***Use your own words:***
_____ Acute/sharp	_____ Itching	____________________
_____ Burning	_____ Numbness	____________________
_____ Shooting	_____ Throbbing	____________________
_____ Hot	_____ Pins and needles	____________________
_____ Tingling	_____ Crippling	____________________
_____ Angry	_____ Dull	____________________
_____ Chapped	_____ Excruciating	____________________
_____ Heavy	_____ Irritated	____________________
_____ Inflamed	_____ Raw	____________________
_____ Swollen	_____ Stabbing	____________________
_____ Vice-like	_____ Stiff	____________________
_____ Tender	_____ Swollen	____________________

C. *Using a picture to describe pain location*: Please put an X on <u>*all*</u> of the parts of the body where you experience pain right now or on a daily or weekly basis. If you wish you can write a word next to the site that describes the type of pain (e.g., the words used in B above).

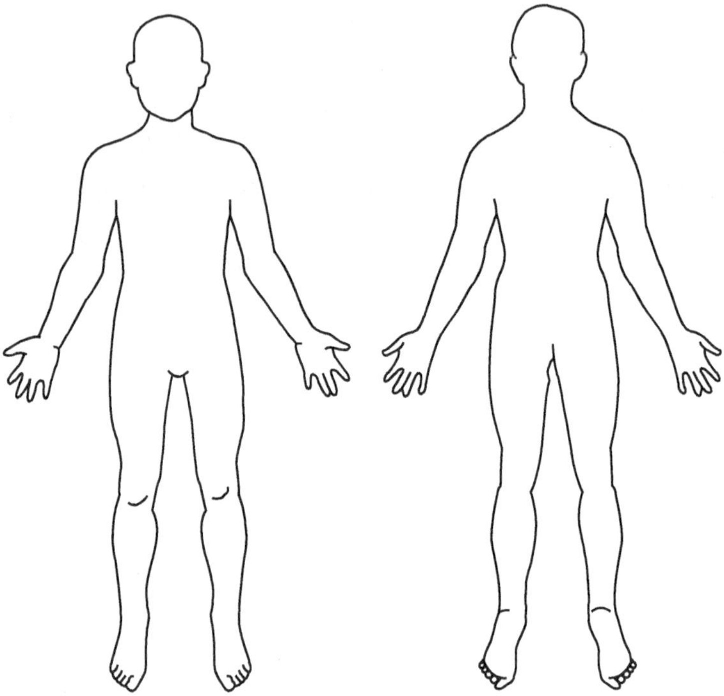

D. *Using a scale to describe the effects of your pain*: Imagine that the pain you are experiencing right now were to continue for several days. What might be your experience on the *third day*?

1 = I am not really aware of the pain unless I choose to focus on it. I can go about my daily activities. The pain is very manageable.

2 = I am not really aware of the pain until I focus on it, but it is affecting my mood. Others might notice my mood or behavior has changed slightly. The pain is manageable.

3 = I am aware of the pain enough that I do some things to accommodate the pain (e.g., shift in chair, take off shoes, stretch, walk around, stop walking). However, I can still go about my daily activities. The pain is still manageable, but there is risk of it becoming less manageable.

4 = The pain is very present, and I have to alter my daily activities to accommodate the pain. I might go home early, rest, change position, put on or take off a brace, use an assistive device more, take medicine to reduce the pain. The pain is unmanageable because it affects my activities too much.

5 = The pain is commanding most or all of my attention. I am stopping my daily activities to make efforts to cope with or reduce the pain. The pain is unmanageable because it is all I can think about.

a. Put a mark on the line that describes the most pain you are experiencing *right now*.

1	2	3	4	5

b. Put a mark on the line that describes the most pain you experienced *yesterday*.

1	2	3	4	5

c. Put a mark on the line that describes what is *most typical* for you when you are going about your daily activities (i.e., there is nothing unusual that you are doing that day that you don't do most days).

1	2	3	4	5

E. Your pain history. Over your entire lifetime, what has been your experience with pain?

What has been the most pain you ever experienced? What were the circumstances of this experience?

____

____

____

____

How did your parents/family respond if you or a sibling were in physical pain?

What messages about pain did you learn from your family (e.g., suck it up; lay low until it passes; soldier on; pamper yourself; suffer in silence; and make sure others know you are in pain)?

Activity 7.3: What Does the Media Talk About When They Talk About Disability?

Activity: Spend 1 week keeping a journal with all references to disability in any media sources: news on any medium, television shows, magazines, billboards, advertisements, movies, traffic reports, Facebook, twitter, Instagram, and more. Go to at least one daily news source each day for 7 days.

Where: At home and online.

Purpose: To notice the messages about disability that are promulgated in various sites throughout all public spaces.

Learning Objectives

1. To increase awareness of how disability is referenced in public spaces.
2. To notice if disability is used as a metaphor and for what purposes.
3. To chronicle if and how disability is a part of public discourse.

Materials: Notebook.

Preparation: Although none is required, two things might help students. The first is a discussion of what constitutes a disability for the purposes of this assignment. A broad definition that includes chronic conditions, such as asthma, diabetes, multiple sclerosis, HIV/AIDS, heart conditions, emphysema, and others, will make it more likely that students will find relevant material. The second is if the instructor brings in some examples before students do this activity, such as a print ad for a medicine for a particular disability, a traffic report that referenced a "disabled vehicle" blocking traffic, or a newspaper article that mentions a subject's disability status.

Time: One week, about 20 minutes per day scattered through the day.

Possible Outcomes: Some students may fail to find anything referencing disability. This is more likely due to not noticing than the total absence of relevant materials, but nonetheless the absence of references can lead to a fruitful discussion.

Talking Points: The words *disability*, *handicap*, *lame*, and *blind* are often used to describe problems: Did students find such examples? Were there any stories about a person with a disability who overcame odds? Did ads for medicine make it seem as if the medicine would erase all problems? What conditions were the targets of the ads? Were actors with disabilities apparent in any films or television shows? (Did the actor truly have a disability?) What were the messages conveyed about disability, and were they consistent or contradictory?

Grading Rubric: 5 points for a notebook with observations and 5 points for up to one page about observations and conclusions.

Handouts: None.

Additional Reading

Brittain, I. (2017). Communicating and managing the message: Media and media representation of disability and paralympic sport. In S. Darcy, S. Frawley, & D. Adair (Eds.), *Managing the Paralympics* (pp.241–262). London: Palgrave Macmillan. https://doi.org/10.1057/978-1-137-43522-4_11

Goethals, T., Mortelmans, D., & Van Hove, G. (2018). Toward a more balanced representation of disability? A content analysis of media coverage in the Flemish print media. *Journal of Human Development, Disability and Social Change, 24*(1), 109–120.

Lu, J., Webber, W., Romero, D., & Chirino, C. (2017). Changing attitudes toward people with disabilities using public media: An experimental study. *Rehabilitation Counseling Bulletin, 61*(3), 175–186.

Rees, L., Robinson, P., & Shields, N. (2019). Media portrayal of elite athletes with disability: A systematic review. *Disability and Rehabilitation, 41*(4), 374–381.

Stewart, K., & Spurgeon, C. (2020). Researching media participation by listing to people with disability. *Media, Culture & Society, 42*(6), 969–986. https://doi.org/10.1177/0163443719890536

Wood, J. F. (2020). Disability in the media: Examining stigma and identity. *Communication Research Trends, 39*(1), 38–39.

8 Watching Films

THERE ARE TWO activities in this chapter. The first has students pick one film from a list and respond to how disability is depicted from several vantage points (e.g., the director, the character, the story). The second activity is best done over 10 weeks, with a sequence of mostly nonfiction films or YouTube videos. These are in the sequence I have used with students—The sequence is not random, but there is nothing holy about the order either. I believe they increase somewhat in complexity of disability messages, but this is not empirically verified. The videos and films should not be rushed through, however, because the idea is to have students take time to reflect as they move through the sequence.

Teaching Disability. Rhoda Olkin, Oxford University Press. © Oxford University Press 2021.
DOI: 10.1093/oso/9780190850661.003.0008

Activity 8.1: Disability in Storytelling

Activity: Watch a film from the list below and then answer questions about the film. Films depict physical, systemic, cognitive, or intellectual disability. Films specifically about mental disorders (of which there are many) are not included in this activity.

Where: At home.

Purpose: To understand how disability is used as a metaphorical device in storytelling.

Learning Objectives

1. To analyze how disability is depicted in the film by the character and by the director.
2. To consider the overriding message about disability by the film as a whole.
3. To categorize films into common tropes about disability.

Materials: Platform on which to watch films.

Preparation: None required. However, having everyone watch the same film and then discussing it in class can help students delve deeper into how disability is used in a film. *Rain Man* is a good film for this, as it includes several aspects to consider: (a) the effects of autism spectrum disorder (ASD) per se versus the effects of long-term institutionalization; (b) family responses; (c) planning for adult children with disabilities after parents are deceased; (d) what supports need to be in place for someone with ASD to live alone; and (e) intersectionality of gender, race/ethnicity, and disability (and note that almost everyone in the film is White).

Time: Length of film plus about 1 to 2 hours to complete the homework.

Possible Outcomes: Some films have "feel good" messages until one drills down on the disability messages. Students with disabilities generally will be able to see more nuances in films than others. Since each student may watch a different film, it is useful to look at the aggregate across all films. Films that promulgate the social model of disability are rare. They are more likely to have more than one character with a disability and to be directed by a person with lived experience of disability.

Talking Points: What model of disability (moral, medical, or social) did the film exemplify? How do movies both reflect and shape social perceptions of disability? Was the disabled character in a romantic relationship? If you as a viewer knew nothing about disability at all, what would you have learned from this film? Was disability presented as a tragedy? In how many films was the disabled character a child rather than an adult? Was the character with a disability depressed or anxious? Did the nondisabled characters gain meaning or learn lessons from the disabled character? Does an able-bodied person rescue the disabled character?

Grading Rubric: 15 points total, 2 points for Questions 1–6 and 3 points for Question 7 on Handout 8.1a.

Handouts: 8.1a: Categories and Questions for Students; 8.1b: List of Films with Disabled Characters.

Additional Reading

Barden, O. (2018). Disability media studies. *Disability & Society, 33*(10), 1672–1674. https://doi.org/10.1080/09687599.2018.1541611

Black, R. S., & Pretes, L. (2007). Victims and victors: Representation of physical disability on the silver screen. *Research and Practice for Persons with Severe Disability, 32*(1), 66–83.

Cuelenaere, E., Willems, G., & Joye, S. (2019). Remaking identities and stereotypes: How film remakes transform and reinforce nationality, disability, and gender. *European Journal of Cultural Studies, 22*(5–6). https://doi.org/10.1177/1367549418821850

D'Souza, R. A., & Rauchberg, J. S. (2019). Neoliberal values and queer/disability in *Margarita with a Straw*. *Journal of International and Intercultural Communication, 13*(2), 183–196.

Kama, A. (2004). Supercrips versus the pitiful handicapped: Reception of disabling images by disabled audience members. *Communications, 29*, 447–466.

Kraeyenoord, C. V. (2011). Movies and disability: Positive impact or harm? *International Journal of Disability, Development and Education, 58*(2), 103–106.

Olkin, R. (2017). D-AT III: Models of disability. In *Disability-affirmative therapy: A case formulation template for clients with disabilities* (Chapter 6). New York: Oxford University Press.

Safran, S. P. (1998). Disability portrayal in film: Reflecting the past, directing the future. *Exceptional Children, 64*(2), 227–238.

See also two documentaries about disability in the movies *CinemAbility* (2013) and *Diffability Hollywood* (2016).

Handout 8.1a: Categories and Questions for Students

Categories of disability depiction in films (students may add others):

a. Disability as emblem of evil;
b. Disability as fate worse than death;
c. People with disabilities as outsiders or "special" (e.g., Special Olympics);
d. Compensation models—as one sense is impaired, another is heightened;
e. Inspirational/feel-good movies, disability empowers and lifts up others;
f. People with disabilities provide valuable lessons for others, make them better people;
g. Person with a disability who is despondent is rescued by able-bodied other(s);
h. Positive depictions of life with a disability;
i. Disability as asexual;
j. Disability as scare tactic or object of pity (e.g., telethons);
k. Disabled people help each other.

Questions

1. Give a brief plot summary.
2. What category (or categories) did this film fit from the list above (or others)?
3. What was the role of the person with the disability in the film, how was that person instrumental in the plot, and what role did disability play?
4. What model of disability was depicted?
5. What was the director's point of view on disability?
6. What was the take-home message the film left the viewer with?
7. Your conclusions.

Handout 8.1b: List of Films with Disabled Characters

Films	
Afraid of the Dark	*Moonstruck*
And the Band Played on	*Mozart and the Whale*
Angels in America	*Murder Ball*
As Good as It Gets	*Music Within*
Best Boy (documentary)	*Musical Chairs*
The Bone Collector	*My Left Foot*
Breathing Lessons	*'Night Mother*
Children of a Lesser God	*Notting Hill*
Coming Home	*Porgy and Bess*
Complaints of a Dutiful Daughter (documentary)	*My Name Is Sam*
Daredevil	*Radio*
Dear Frankie	*Rain Man*
Diving Bell and the Butterfly	*Riding the Bus with My Sister*
Dominick and Eugene	*Rory O'Shea Was Here*
Edward Scissorhands	*Rust and Bone*
Extremely Loud and Incredibly Close	*Scent of a Woman*
Forrest Gump	*The Sea Inside*
I Am Sam	*Simon Burch*
Inside Moves	*Station Agent*
Long Ago, Tomorrow	*Waterdance*
Looking for Mr. Goodbar (Note: violence)	*Where Hope Grows*
Mask	*Whose Life Is It Anyway?*
Million Dollar Baby	

Activity 8.2: Film Immersion

Activity: Watch a series of films in a *10-week sequence* designed to get more immersed in insiders' views of living with various types of disabilities and write responses to each film.

Where: At home on computer or streaming device.

Purpose: To gain an understanding of various disabilities from insiders' perspectives and to stay immersed in the disability world over a period of time.

Learning Objectives

1. To become aware of ways that people with disabilities talk about their own disabilities.
2. To increase understanding of the importance for people with disabilities of affiliation with a disability culture and community.
3. To become familiar with some specific disabilities.
4. To experience increasing levels of understanding of disability as a dimension of diversity rather than as a pathology.

Materials: Access to YouTube and streaming sites (URLs are listed).

Preparation: No preparation is required, but students should be cautioned that rushing through films at a faster pace than weekly will inhibit their learning. Changing viewpoints takes time and thought and going from film to film without time in between diminishes depth of understanding.

Time: 10 weeks, approximately 2 hours/week.

Possible Outcomes: Feedback from students as they move through the sequence may be helpful in pinpointing which films have more impact and provide information about maximizing the sequence. Some issues that will be very obvious to students with disabilities (e.g., language usage and the need for adaptive day care for children with disabilities) will be new to those without disabilities. Different students will react uniquely to the films, but some responses will be common, and illuminating both of these in class discussions is helpful. The color blindness tests (Week 7) may yield some new diagnoses.

Talking Points: Which films had more or less impact? Did understanding of one type of disability (e.g., Tourette syndrome) generalize to other types of disabilities, or was it necessary to learn about categories of disabilities (e.g., visual impairments)?

How did reactions to films change over time? What about the order of films: Were there some that should have been sooner/later in the sequence? What specifically did you learn that will translate into concrete behaviors with clients with disabilities?

Grading Rubric: Film reaction papers, maximum of 1 page per week, 2 points each, for a total of 20 points.

Handouts: 8.2: List of YouTube Links and Films.

Additional Reading

Dunn, D. S., & Andrews, E. E. (2015). Person-first and identity-first language: Developing psychologists' cultural competence using disability language. *American Psychologist, 70*(3), 255–264. http://dx.doi.org/10.1037/a0038636

Masters, J. (2015). Hollywood in the classroom: Using feature films to teach. *Nurse Educator, 30*(3), 113–116. (*Note*: Includes a 12-item scale to assess students' beliefs about the value of films as a learning experience.)

Nittoli, J. M. (2017). Using popular film to teach multicultural counseling: A constructivist approach. *Journal of Creativity in Mental Health, 13*(3), 344–357. https://doi.org/10.1080/15401383.2017.1340216

Olkin, R., & Pledger, C. (2003). Can disability studies and psychology join hands? *American Psychologist, 58*(4), 296–304.

Handout 8.2: List of YouTube Links and Films

1. *Disability rights movement:* https://www.youtube.com/watch?v=SyWcCuVta7M; and *Ed Roberts: Free Wheeling*: https://www.youtube.com/watch?v=ci3ek-tqiGQ
2. *Overcoming Ableism*: https://www.youtube.com/watch?v=X1xnyVCBYNQ; and Fighting for disability rights: https://www.youtube.com/watch?v=ABFpTRlJUuc
3. *Able Privilege* (Alan Larson): https://www.youtube.com/watch?v=mX9tgr7yfwo; and National MS Society: *Invisible Symptoms*: https://www.youtube.com/watch?v=vqUN77VdI-s
4. Six YouTube videos:
   a. Parents with disabilities: https://www.youtube.com/watch?v=tP8yJJMoNgo (5 minutes)
   https://www.youtube.com/watch?v=rYHCyVFd2AQ (17 minutes)
   https://www.youtube.com/watch?v=kawZfSpOrPY (26 minutes)
   b. Jalen: https://www.youtube.com/watch?v=FPxPPgVWbmY
   c. Single mom: https://www.youtube.com/watch?v=JrRBrX8YxFs (8 minutes)
   d. Adapted daycare: https://www.youtube.com/watch?v=q9y3WBKVCGA (3 minutes)
   e. Hannah and Shane I: https://www.youtube.com/watch?v=f8Gub_g__Dw (7½ minutes)
   f. Hannah and Shane II: https://www.youtube.com/watch?v=uxohUoxUk_Y (5½ minutes)
5. Films about intersectionality (gay and disabled) and devotees:
   a. *I'm Gay and Disabled and Fine*: https://www.youtube.com/watch?v=ZZUmUgmc5PE (*Caution:* very explicit language) (4 minutes)
   b. Queer bear in a chair: https://www.youtube.com/watch?v=glMN_F_Z6qM (4 minutes)
   c. Devotees: https://www.youtube.com/watch?v=9FAhMbtqcNo (25 minutes, then it seems to repeat)
6. Deaf Culture:
   a. *Deaf Culture Is Shifting*: https://www.youtube.com/watch?v=wLDM2pPYoOs (5 minutes)
   b. *Protecting and Interpreting Deaf Culture*: https://www.youtube.com/watch?v=io7z5PftOU4 (16 minutes)

   c. Sound and Fury—Cochlear Implants: Available on hulu, amazon prime video (1 hour 18 minutes)
      Alternative choice, TED talk by Deaf woman navigating both Deaf and hearing worlds: https://www.youtube.com/watch?v=jhm5OaXJVMQ (14 minutes)
7. Tourette syndrome; blindness and visual impairments:
   a. *Twitch and Shout*: https://documentary.net/video/tourette-syndrome/ (42 minutes)
   b. *How Blind People Actually See the World*: https://www.youtube.com/watch?v=VN3U1MWJsdo (7½ minutes)
   c. *Blind People Tell Us Which Questions Annoy Them the Most*: https://www.youtube.com/watch?v=_oVR8NcKJoY (5 minutes)
   d. *How Color Blindness Works*: https://www.youtube.com/watch?v=iNRQB5309yo (6½ minutes)
   e. *Color Blind Test*: https://www.youtube.com/watch?v=emEKDwwoiac (5 minutes) (*If interested in further testing your own color vision, google the Farnsworth-Munson color test.*)
8. *Little People of America:* https://www.youtube.com/watch?v=3rRCToJzUiw (57 minutes)
9. *Miss You Can Do It Pageant*: https://www.youtube.com/watch?v=4zthRVzojlQ (22 minutes)
10. *Things People with Disabilities Wish You Knew*: https://www.youtube.com/watch?v=_b7k6pEnyQ4 (5 minutes)

C More Advanced Exercises

THIS SECTION HAS two chapters and twelve activities, addressing disability in the context of family, friends, work, and community. There is now more focus than the beginning exercises on how those with disabilities interact with the real world. Chapter 9 has five activities, including how one's living space might have to be modified, the necessary steps to assure accessibility before leaving home, and finding a map for handicapped parking in your own community. Then intersectionality is addressed in parts I (religion) and II (multiple marginalized identities). In this chapter a focus is on the ways one navigates the immediate environment, and the extra tasks imposed on disabled people in living and negotiating that environment.

Chapter 10 dives deeper into disability experience in seven activities. The first two activities are about how disability-related fatigue impacts daily life, ways to manage it, and the choices one has to make to accommodate fatigue. The next activity is about being an outsider as an able-bodied person, by attending an event where most people have disabilities. This flips the usual scenario whereby persons with disabilities are the outsiders, and often are highly visible as *the* disabled person.

Microaggressions are very relevant for disabled people, yet these microaggressions are often hidden to others or even disbelieved by others ("no one would do that!"). One activity has students asking a disabled person about their experiences of microaggressions. When these are shared across a classroom it becomes apparent that microaggressions are a very frequent – and often highly disturbing – occurrence.

Another activity has participants watch a live TV show such as the news with closed captioning. A comparison of what is spoken versus what is captured in text is enlightening of how much those who are Deaf or hard-of-hearing miss. After making this comparison, watching with the sound off can be illuminating as well.

The next activity asks students to become change agents for a disability issue of their choosing by researching the issue and writing to the appropriate official requesting specific changes. The philosophy behind this activity is that clinicians have a role in making life easier for marginalized persons that goes beyond the therapy room.

The last activity includes clinical vignettes. Since one ultimate goal of this book is not only to change attitudes and increase knowledge, but to improve skills and cultural responsivity to clients with disabilities, it is fitting that the final activity focuses on clients with disabilities. There are many ways the vignettes can be used, and this activity could be stretched out over time, with other activities and readings in between, to promote overall depth of understanding by students as they move through the vignettes.

9 Disability in the Context of Family, Friends, and Community

CHAPTER 9 HAS five activities. The first three are about living independently and with full inclusion from your personal abode to the community. The next two activities focus on intersectionality (Parts II and III; Part I was in Chapter 3).

Teaching Disability. Rhoda Olkin, Oxford University Press. © Oxford University Press 2021.
DOI: 10.1093/oso/9780190850661.003.0009

Activity 9.1: Evaluate Your Dwelling for Accessibility

Activity: Consider all aspects of the place where you live and what would have to change to be completely wheelchair accessible, who has the responsibility to make changes, and what the approximate costs would be.

Where: At home, on computer, and on phone.

Purpose: To understand one of the hidden costs of disability: the need to modify one's residence and the considerable time and costs of doing so.

Learning Objectives

1. To know how to evaluate a dwelling for wheelchair accessibility.
2. To delineate modifications needed.
3. To understand responsibilities of landlords versus renters.
4. To approximate costs of modifications.
5. To learn what agencies can be of assistance in the process.

Materials: Tape measure (12 feet or longer), Evaluation Checklist (Handout 9.1b).

Preparation: Students generally will be familiar with obvious accessibility issues such as ramps versus stairs but unfamiliar with other types of issues, such as knee space, faucet handles, grab bars, slope of ramps, and more. It can be useful to brainstorm the kinds of modifications that are typical and to review the guidelines at the U.S. Department of Justice 2010 ADA Standards for Accessible Design. A walk around campus pointing out wheelchair accommodations can raise awareness before doing the assignment. Of note is how bicycles and wheelchairs often compete for the same spaces.

Time: Approximately 4 hours, excluding class time.

Possible Outcomes: Students may find this assignment somewhat difficult as information is not always easily found. They will discover that modifications are costly and usually require hiring a professional for installation. Landlords have to permit modifications but also are allowed to require that modifications be removed if the person moves out. There are disadvantages to moving as some modifications are structural and cannot accompany the person with the disability to the new abode. Makeshift modifications may serve for a time but generally are not durable and may be unsafe.

Talking Points: Accommodations for one type of disability can be the opposite for another type of disability; did this come up? How easy or hard was it to find the regulations for specific modifications (e.g., turning radius, slope of a ramp, width of inside and outside doors)? What modifications were relatively inexpensive? Which were the most expensive? Could any be done by a handy person without hiring a contractor? What were the responsibilities of a landlord?

Grading Rubric: This is a longer assignment and should receive more points than other assignments. I suggest 5 points for a list of modifications needed, 10 points for the appropriate modifications, 5 points for estimated costs, and 5 points for the report, for a total of 25 points.

Handouts: 9.1a: Instructions for Students; 9.1b: Evaluation Checklist.

Additional Reading

Eid, M. A., Giakoumidisi, N., & El Saddik, A. (2016). A novel eye-gaze-controlled wheelchair system for navigating unknown environments: Case study with a person with ALS. *IEEE Access, 4*, 558–575. https://doi.org/10.1109/ACCESS.2016.2520093

Lynch, S., & Hill, J. (2020). "I had to pop a wheelie and pay extra attention in order not to fall": Embodied experiences of two wheelchair tennis athletes transgressing ableist and gendered norms in disability sport and university spaces. *Qualitative Research in Sport, Exercise and Health*. https://doi.org/10.1080/2159676X.2020.1731575

Mohanta, M., Reddy, M. V., & Lakshmi, Y. V. (2017). Barriers in the homes of wheelchair users. *Research Inspiration, 2*(3), 163–172. https://www.researchgate.net/profile/Vvijaya_Lakshmi/publication/324496163_BARRIERS_IN_THE_HOMES_OF_WHEELCHAIR_USERS/links/5ad05c5faca2723a3346ade1/BARRIERS-IN-THE-HOMES-OF-WHEELCHAIR-USERS.pdf

Morales, E., Gamache, S., Routhier, F., Rousseau, J., & Doyle, O. (2018). Pilot study to measure wheelchair users' space requirements in the bathroom. *Journal of Enabling Technologies, 12*(3), 129–140. https://doi.org/10.1108/JET-02-2018-0007

Sung, J., Trace, Y., Peterson, E., Sosnoff, J. J., & Rice, L. A. (2019). Falls among full-time wheelchair users with spinal cord injury and multiple sclerosis: A comparison of characteristics of fallers and circumstances of falls. *Disability and Rehabilitation, 41*(4), 389–395. https://doi.org/10.1080/09638288.2017.1393111

Handout 9.1a: Instructions for Students

For this assignment, you will (a) evaluate your current dwelling for wheelchair accessibility (see Handout 9.1b for a helpful checklist) and (b) make a list of all the modifications that would be needed. If you are a renter, (c) note which of these would be the landlord's responsibility (i.e., all modifications outside the front door of your apartment/condominium). (d) To determine an appropriate modification, consult federal standards and your state guidelines (see below for useful websites). (e) Estimate the cost of making the three most important modifications. (f) Write a one-page report of your results and attach the completed checklist and the names of any websites or agencies you consulted.

Helpful Information

For federal information:

- U.S. Department of Justice 2010 ADA Standards for Accessible Design
- U.S. Department of Justice Revised (2010) ADA Regulations Implementing Title II and Title III

For guidance on how to find information for your state, here is where the information is for California. It will be different for every state.

The California Commission on Disability Access: https://www.dgs.ca.gov/CCDA/Resources

The Department of General Services has a resources tab with access compliance reference materials. For example, information about making forms accessible: https://www.dgs.ca.gov/Resources/Statewide-Forms/ADAComplianceToolkit

The Division of State Architect develops and maintains accessibility standards and is housed under the Department of General Services (https://www.dgs.ca.gov/DSA/contact).

The Department of Rehabilitation Services (https://www.dor.ca.gov) has Title 24 of the California Code regulations and the Division of the State Architects Access Compliance Reference Manual.

Handout 9.1b: Evaluation Checklist

Yes means good accessibility; *No* means there is a problem that impedes accessibility.

Outside Approach	**Yes No**	**Unsure**	**Comments**
Gate and curb cuts			
Steps			
Railing/bannister			
Parking			
Direct access from parking			
Paving and ramps			
Front or side door entry			
Automatic door openers			
Living Areas			
Adequate space to get around			
Can get to windows			
Windows operable from wheelchair			
Light switches accessible			
Outlets accessible			
Doorways sufficiently wide			
Kitchen			
Entryway wide enough			
Knee space below sink			
Knee space below counters			
Counter space at good height			
Can access storage cabinets			

Circulation space to access areas			
Refrigerator opens in good direction			
Can access refrigerator and freezer			
Accessible light switches			
Accessible outlets			
Bathroom			
Doorway wide enough			
Can enter and close door			
Knee space under faucet			
Faucet reachable			
Single lever for water			
Mirror at right height			
Towel accessible			
Light switch and outlets accessible			
Storage for items accessible			
Safety grab bars			
Tub or shower modifications			
Nonslip flooring and mats			

Activity 9.2: Check Accessibility Everywhere Before You Go

Activity: For 1 week before leaving the house, call to inquire about accessibility for every destination for that day, even if you have been there before, and record results.

Where: In the community.

Purpose: To illuminate the extra burden placed on people with disabilities because disability accessibility cannot be assumed and to note which places in the community are and are not accessible. To illustrate that being able to get in the door (or a different door) is not the same as being fully included.

Learning Objectives

1. Learn what questions to ask to ascertain "disability accessibility."
2. Gain experience in one of the hidden burdens placed on people with disabilities.
3. Describe the accessibility of your community.
4. Explore the difference between access and full inclusion.

Materials: Recording Sheet (Handout 9.2b).

Preparation: If students have not been assigned a disability (see Activity 3.2, Handout 3.2a for a list of possible disabilities), assign each student one of three choices: wheelchair user (either electric or manual); limited mobility (with crutches, cane, or walker); or blindness. For the first two groups, students should carry a stick with them at all times to remind them that at least one hand will always be busy with a mobility device. Students can then work in small groups in or outside class to generate the questions they would need to ask to evaluate accessibility. (Handout 9.1b might be helpful in this regard.)

Time: 40 minutes in small group to generate questions and start to fill out the Recording Sheet (Handout 9.2b), and seven full days to do the assignment.

Possible Outcomes: Undoubtedly, students will discover they need to add items to the recording sheet as they go. For example, they may remember to ask about parking and a ramped or level entrance but forget to ask about the restroom.

Talking Points: Since the Americans with Disabilities Act was passed in 1990, why is it that a person still cannot assume disability accessibility? What community, county, state, and federal agencies are responsible for addressing inaccessibility? How much of a burden was it to check for accessibility all week long? Were any friends' houses wheelchair accessible? What accommodations does a blind person need? Are any of these a problem for someone with a different kind of disability?

Grading Rubric: 10 points: 1 point per day for 7 days, plus 3 points for final report.

Handouts: 9.2a: Instructions for Students; 9.2b: Recording Sheet.

Additional Reading

Baker, S. M., Stephens, D. L., & Hill, R. P. (2001). Marketplace experiences of individuals with visual impairments: Beyond the Americans with Disabilities Act. *Business Faculty Publications and Presentations, 3*. http://pilotscholars.up.edu/bus_facpubs/3

Befort, S. F. (2013). An empirical analysis of case outcomes under the ADA Amendments Act, 70 Wash. & Lee L. Rev. 2027. https://scholarship.law.umn.edu/faculty_articles/114

Crossley, M. (2017). Community integration of people with disabilities: Can *Olmstead* protect against retrenchment? *Laws, 6*(4), 22–34.

Enyart, S. (2020). Reflections on the 30th anniversary of the Americans with Disabilities Act of 1990: What has the blind and low vision community gained? *Journal of Visual Impairment and Blindness, 114*(1), 73–76. https://doi.org/10.1177/0145482X19901020

Eyer, K. (2012). That's not discrimination: American beliefs and the limits of anti-discrimination law. *Minnesota Law Review, 407*. https://www.minnesotalawreview.org/wp-content/uploads/2019/07/Eyer_MLR1275.pdf

Sabat, D., Richarson, M., Matrone, K., Umbarger, D., & Weaver, A. (2017). Community engagement in health care: An approach to improve health care access for people with disabilities. *Disability Studies Quarterly, 37*(3). http://dx.doi.org/10.18061/dsq.v37i3.5254

Victor, C. M., Thacker, L. R., Gary, K. W., Pawluk, D., & Capolillo, A. (2017). Workplace discrimination and visual impairment: A comparison of Equal Employment Opportunity Commission charges and resolutions under the Americans with Disabilities Amendments Act. *Journal of Visual Impairment and Blindness, 111*(5), 475–482.

White, G. W., & Summers, J. A. (2017). People with disabilities and community participation. *Journal of Prevention and Intervention in the Community, 45*(2), 81–85. https://doi.org/10.1080/10852352.2017.1281041

Handout 9.2a: Instructions for Students

1. You have been assigned a disability related to wheelchair use, mobility impairment, or blindness.
2. For the next week, starting tomorrow morning, you will call before you leave the house to ascertain accessibility of your destination(s). For example, if you are going to a restaurant and you are "blind," you might ask about the nearest public transportation spot, whether there is a menu in Braille, whether there is a good spot under the table for your guide dog, if someone in the kitchen or the waiter will cut the meat for you before serving, and if the restrooms have Braille signage. If you are going to a big box store and you have limited mobility, you might ask about the number of handicapped parking spaces and the times of day they tend to be available, whether the restroom is slippery, if there is a stall for a person with a handicap, and if the faucets have single handles.
3. Carry a stick with you at all times. If you are a wheelchair user, this is to remind you that you need a hand free to run the electric wheelchair tiller or two hands to power the manual wheelchair. If you are mobility impaired, the stick is a stand-in for crutches, cane, or walker. If you are blind, the stick is either a guide dog or white cane. The stick must be either in your hand or near you at all times.
4. Go about your week, but before you leave to go anywhere, call your destination to inquire about accessibility. Record responses and the actual degree of accessibility that you find on the recording sheet (Handout 9.2b).
5. Write a one-page report at the end of the week about your experiences. Attach your recording sheet to the report.

Handout 9.2b: Recording Sheet

Date	Destination	Questions	Accuracy	Forgot to Ask	Problems

Activity 9.3: A Map to Your Community

Activity: Find the name and contact information for the 504 coordinator for your town/city; request a map of handicapped parking in your town/city, then assess the map and provide feedback regarding its accuracy, readability, utility, whether it is up to date, and if it is available in alternate formats for those who are blind or have low vision.

Where: On the phone and Internet.

Purpose: To become familiar with how to find handicapped parking in your locale and to assess any existing map of handicapped parking.

Learning Objectives

1. To understand the role of a 504 coordinator for a locale.
2. To know how to access specific information related to handicapped parking.
3. To assess the utility of a map that includes handicapped parking.
4. To make suggestions to improve the utility of the map.

Materials: None.

Preparation: Reading about the Rehabilitation Act of 1973 (implemented in 1975) is helpful but not necessary. Students need to know that this act's Section 504 is related to public access, and that every municipality has a person who coordinates information about public access. Searching a city's website should yield the contact information for this person.

Time: 2 hours.

Possible Outcomes: It is probable that the city has a map of handicapped parking, but there may be problems with the map in that it might (a) be very tiny and hard to read; (b) list locations of handicapped parking but not the number of spots in each location; (c) not differentiate between public and private parking; (d) cover only business (not residential) areas of the city or the downtown only; (e) include lots of other information so that the handicapped parking is hard to see.

Talking Points: How easy or difficult was it to find the contact information for the 504 coordinator? Was the student able to contact that person? Did a map of handicapped parking exist, and was it available either to everyone (online) or by request? Imagine a person with a cognitive or learning disability: How clear and comprehensible was the map? What would improve the utility of the map?

Grading Rubric: 5 points for locating the 504 coordinator and a map of handicapped parking; 5 points for assessment of the map and specific suggestions for improvement.

Handouts: 9.3a: Instructions for Students: 9.3b: Example Map of One Town in California.

Additional Reading

Fletcher, D. (2001). A guilt gradient in the illegal use of parking spaces reserved for people with disabilities: Field observations over five years. *Perceptual and Motor Skills, 93*(1), 157–162. https://doi.org/10.2466/pms.2001.93.1.157

Miller, G. P., & Singer, L. S. (2000). Handicapped parking. *Hofstra Law Review, 29*(1), 81–126. http://scholarlycommons.law.hofstra.edu/hlr/vol29/iss1/2

Paradis, L. (2003). Title II of the Americans with Disabilities Act and Section 504 of the Rehabilitation Act: Making programs, services, and activities accessible for all. *Stanford Law & Policy Review, 14*, 389.

Weber, M. C. (1995). Disability discrimination by state and local government: The relationship between Section 504 of the Rehabilitation Act and Title II of the Americans with Disabilities Act. *William and Mary Law Review, 36*(3), 1089–1133.

Handout 9.3a: Instructions for Students

Starting in 1975 under the Rehabilitation Act, Section 504, any place or entity receiving federal funding must be accessible to people with disabilities. This includes virtually every town and city in the United States. Thus, municipalities created a position of 504 coordinator (though it might go by other names such as disability or accessibility coordinator).

1. Your task is to find the person responsible for overseeing compliance in your area. If your town and county are one and the same (e.g., San Francisco is both a city and comprises the entire San Francisco County), there will be one person for the county. Otherwise, there likely will be a designated person for each town or city.
2. When you contact the 504 coordinator, request a map of all handicapped parking in your town. It might be emailed to you or available on the town's website.
3. Using the map, go to several of the places designated as handicapped parking. Observe how easy or difficult it is to find the designated spots.
4. Write a brief report noting the following: Was the map (a) very tiny and hard to read; (b) a list of locations of handicapped parking but without the number of spots in each location; (c) not differentiated by public and private parking; (d) only for business (not residential) areas of the city or the downtown only; (e) crowded with lots of other information so that the handicapped parking is hard to see.
5. Write to the 504 coordinator with recommendations for improvements to the map. (Turn in a copy of the letter to your instructor.)

Handout 9.3b: Map of One Town's Handicapped Parking

Activity 9.4: Intersectionality (Part II)—Religion

Activity: Explore what your own (or your assigned) religion says about disability.

Where: Research and PowerPoint preparation done at home, presentation in class.

Purpose: To explore commonalities and differences across various religions in how disability is conceptualized and what advice it gives about how to treat people with disabilities.

Learning Objectives

1. To explore how religion shapes our views of health, wellness, and disability.
2. To utilize the three main models of disability (moral, medical, social) to understand how disability is framed by various religions.
3. To compare perspectives across religions.

Materials: Students will need access to the main text for their religion (e.g., Koran, Old or New Testament) and other research materials. Access to a leader in their religious community will be helpful.

Preparation: Assign a religion to each student; it will be more meaningful if students select the religion in which they were raised or to which they now subscribe. For students without an affiliation, assign a religion not already being researched (e.g., Unitarian, Quaker, Buddhism, Baptist, Islam). If students share a religion, the instructor can decide to have them work in teams of two or three. However, distinctions should be made within a religion when there are variations (e.g., Jewish orthodox vs. conservative or reform; Episcopalian vs. Roman Catholic).

Time: 20 minutes in class to assign religions. Four weeks to do the research and prepare a presentation. One class period (3 hours) to have student presentations and discussion.

Possible Outcomes: It may not be straightforward to find information specific to disability in original texts; thus, some questions for a leader of the religion may be a good place to start. Texts *about* a religion should be consulted as well as primary treatises. Typing in "[name of religion, e.g., Judaism]" and "disability" into Google Scholar generally yields material. See also the references in Additional Reading.

Talking Points: Students may need guidance to think about the models of disability (see Chapter 6) and their selected religion. For example, Islam talks about kindness and charity to people with disabilities—what does this represent? Are there any similarities or key differences in how the religion conceptualizes the role of women versus people with disabilities? Have viewpoints changed over the centuries? How do students feel about what they have learned?

Grading Rubric: 15 points for presentation: clarity, thoroughness, accuracy, engaging presentation, sticking to time limits.

Handouts: None.

Additional Reading

Al-Aoufi, H., Al-Zyoud, N., & Shahminan, N. (2012). Islam and the cultural conceptualisation of disability. *International Journal of Adolescence and Youth, 17*(4), 205–219.

Chen, L. (2020). Disability theology despite itself. *Journal of Disability & Religion, 24*(4), 393–412. https://www.tandfonline.com/doi/abs/10.1080/23312521.2020.1750531

Claassens, L. J., Shaikh, S., & Swartz, L. (2019). Engaging disability and religion in the global south. In B. Watermeyer, J. McKenzie, & L. Swartz (Eds.), *The Palgrave handbook of disability and citizenship in the global south* (pp. 147–164). New York: Palgrave Macmillan.

Leyser, Y. (1994). Stress and adaptation in orthodox Jewish families with a disabled child. *American Journal of Orthopsychiatry, 63*(3), 376–385.

Mackelprang, R. W., & Salsgiver, R. O. (2002). Religion, spirituality, and clinical practice. *SCI Psychosocial Process, 15*(2), 97–100.

Maysaa, B., & Hatab, T. (2005). Disability in the Qur'an. *Journal of Religion, Disability and Health, 9*(1), 5–27.

Miles, M. (2002). Some historical texts on disability in the classical Muslim world. *Journal of Religion, Disability and Health, 6*(2–3), 77–88.

Musse, I. A. (2001). Disability: An Islamic insight. http://www.naseeb.com/villages/journals/article-from-australia-on-disability-and-islam-5380

O'Hanlon, E. E. (2013). Religion and disability: The experiences of families of children with special needs. *Journal of Religion, Disability & Health, 17*(1), 42–61. https://doi.org/10.1080/15228967.2012.731874

Olyan, S. M. (2008). *Disability and the Hebrew Bible: Interpreting mental and physical difference.* Cambridge, UK: Cambridge University Press.

Otieno, P. A. (2009). Biblical and theological perspectives on disability: Implications on the rights of persons with disability in Kenya. *Disability Studies Quarterly, 29*(4), np. https://dsq-sds.org/article/view/988/1164

Raphael, R. (2008). *Biblical corpora: Representations of disability in Hebrew biblical literature.* New York: T & T Clark.

Rose, A. (1997). Who causes the blind to see: Disability and quality of religious life. *Disability and Society, 12*(3), 395–405.

Schuelka, M. J. (2013). A faith in humanness: Disability, religion and development. *Disability & Society, 28*(4), 500–513. https://doi.org/10.1080/09687599.2012.717880

Stewart, D. T. (2011). Sexual disabilities in the Hebrew Bible. In C. R. Moss & J. Schipper (Eds.), *Disability studies and biblical literature* (pp. 71–72). New York: Palgrave Macmillan.

Strauss, R. P. (1988). Genetic counseling in the cross cultural context: The case of highly observant Judaism. *Patient Education and Counseling, 11*, 43–52.

Swinton, J. (2012). From inclusion to belonging: A practical theology of community, disability and humanness. *Journal of Religion, Disability & Health, 16*(2), 172–190. https://doi.org/10.1080/15228967.2012.676243

Treloar, L. L. (2002). Disability, spiritual beliefs, and the church: The experience of adults with disabilities and family members. *Journal of Advanced Nursing, 40*(5), 594–604.

White, K., & Shernock, J. (2005). Our clients and their religion. *The Therapist, 17*(2), 54–57.

Activity 9.5: Intersectionality (Part III): Multiple Marginalized Identities

Activity: Researching about disability status in the context of other marginalized characteristics and creating a PowerPoint presentation for the class.

Where: Research and creation of PowerPoint presentation at home, presentation in class.

Purpose: To highlight that disability is never a stand-alone feature but part of the totality of a person, all of which must be considered holistically when treating clients with disabilities.

Learning Objectives

1. To synthesize information about two or more marginalized statuses, one of which is disability.
2. To create a PowerPoint in which key information about intersectionality is condensed.
3. To examine key factors that might arise with clients with intersectional identities.

Materials: Internet access; PowerPoint.

Preparation: Students select which topics to research (see Handout 9.5a for possible selections). Not all possible intersectionalities are listed, so students may select something not on the list that represents their own identities. It is desirable that students inhabit one of the two characteristics they are researching so that lived experience can inform their work. For example, a Chinese student could research Chinese and disabled. (*Note: Do not lump all Asian groups together as there are important distinctions across Asian cultures.*)

Time: 20 minutes in class to assign religions. Four weeks to do the research and prepare a presentation. One class period (3 hours) to have student presentations and discussion.

Possible Outcomes: Information on intersectionality when one characteristic is disability can be hard to locate. Much of the literature is opinion rather than empirical and often focuses on rehabilitation outcomes and not general outpatient clinical settings. Furthermore, studies that are empirical that include demographic information about their participants rarely analyze the data separately for diverse groups.

Talking Points: There are varying degrees of stigma attached to different marginalized groups: How does this manifest for the chosen topic? What are the effects on day-to-day living of each identity? How prominent and readily accessible are the communities for each identity? Might the person be an outsider no matter which group they affiliate with, due to the other aspect of their identities? Why do some topics have much more professional literature than others?

Grading Rubric: 15 points for presentation: clarity, thoroughness, accuracy, engaging presentation, sticking to time limits.

Handouts: 9.5a: Possible Topics; 9.5b: Instructions for Students.

Additional Reading

Ali, Z., Fazil, Q., Bywaters, P., Wallace, L., & Singh, G. (2001). Disability, ethnicity and childhood: A critical review of research. *Disability and Society, 16*(7), 949–968.

Alston, R. J. (2004). African Americans with disabilities and the Social Security Administration's return-to-work incentives: A potential clash of culture and policy. *Journal of Disability Policy Studies, 14*(4), 126–221.

Anastasiou, D., Kauffman, J. M., & Michail, D. (2016). Disability in multicultural theory: Conceptual and social justice issues. *Journal of Disability Policy Studies, 27*(1), 3–12.

Arango-Lasprilla, J. C., Ketchum, J. M., Flores Stevens, L., Balcazar, F., Wehman, P., Forster, L., & Hsu, N. (2009). Ethnic/racial differences in employment outcomes following spinal cord injury. *Neurorehabilitation, 24*, 37–46.

Balcazar, F. E., Keys, C. B., & Suarez-Balcazar, Y. (2001). Empowering Latinos with disabilities to address issues of independent living and disability rights: A capacity-building approach. *Journal of Prevention and Intervention in the Community, 21*(2), 53–70.

Banks, M. E., Brown, K. S., Mona, L. R., & Ackerman, R. J. (2015). *Women with disabilities: Affirmative practice and assessment.* In C. Zerbe Enns, J. K. Rice, & R. L. Nutt (Eds.), *Psychology of women book series. Psychological practice with women: Guidelines, diversity, empowerment* (pp. 159–190). American Psychological Association. https://doi.org/10.1037/14460-007

Chen, R. K., Jo, S.-J., & Donnell, C. M. (2004). Enhancing the rehabilitation counseling process: Understanding the obstacles to Asian Americans' utilization of services. *Journal of Applied Rehabilitation Counseling, 35*(1), 7 pgs. http://www.ntac.hawaii.edu/AAPIcourse/downloads/readings/pdf/EnhancingRehab.pdf

Choi, K., & Wynne, M. (2000). Providing services to Asian Americans with developmental disabilities and their families: Mainstream service providers' perspective. *Community Mental Health Journal, 36*(6), 589–595.

Correa, V. I., Bonilla, Z. E., & Reyes-MacPherson, M. E. (2010). Support networks of single Puerto Rican mothers of children with disabilities. *Journal of Child and Family Studies, 20*, 66–77.

Dyches, T. T., Wilder, L. K., Sudweeks, R. R., Obiakor, F. E., & Algozzine, B. (2004). Multicultural issues in autism. *Journal of Autism and Developmental Disorders, 34*(2), 211–222.

Fisher, L., Chesla, C. A., Chun, K. M., Skaff, M. M., Mullan, J. T., & Kanter, R. A. (2004). Patient-appraised couple emotion management and disease management among Chinese American patients with type 2 diabetes. *Journal of Family Psychology, 18*(2), 302–310.

Fredriksen-Goldsen, K. I., Kim, H.-J., & Barkan, S. E. (2012). Disability among lesbian, gay, and bisexual adults: Disparities in prevalence and risk. *American Journal of Public Health, 102*(1), 16–21.

Guter, B., & Killacky, J. R. (Eds., 2004), *Queer crips: Disabled gay men and their stories.* New York: Harrington Park Press.

Harley, D. A., Hall, M., & Savage, T. A. (2000). Working with gay and lesbian consumers with disabilities: Helping practitioners understand another frontier of diversity. *Journal of Applied Rehabilitation Counseling, 31*(1), 4–11.

Hunt, B., Matthews, C., Milsom, A., & Lammel, J. (2006). Lesbians with physical disabilities: A qualitative study of their experiences. *Journal of Counseling & Development, 84*, 163–173.

Hunt, B., Milsom, A., & Matthews, C. (2009). Partner-related rehabilitation experiences of lesbians with physical disabilities. *Rehabilitation Counseling Bulletin, 52*(3), 167–178.

Jarama, S. L., Reyst, H., Rodriguez, M., Belgrave, F. Z., & Zea, M. C. (1998). Psychosocial adjustment among Central American immigrants with disabilities: An exploratory study. *Cultural Diversity and Mental Health, 4*(2), 115–125.

Jones, L., Atkin, K., & Ahmad, W. I. U. (2001). Supporting Asian deaf young people and their families: The role of professionals and services. *Disability and Society, 16*(1), 51–70.

Kim, H.-J., & Fredrickson-Goldsen, K. I. (2012). Hispanic lesbians and bisexual women at heightened risk or health disparities. *American Journal of Public Health, 102*(1), 9–15.

Koca-Atabey, M., Nuray Karanci, A. N., Dirik, G., & Aydemir, D. (2011). Psychological wellbeing of Turkish university students with physical impairments: An evaluation within the stress-vulnerability paradigm. *International Journal of Psychology, 46*(2), 106–118.

Marshall, C. A. (Ed.) (2001). Rehabilitation and American Indians with disabilities: A handbook for administrators, practitioners, and researchers. *Rehabilitation Education, 16*(1), 103–104.

McDonald, K. E., Keys, C. B., & Balcazar, F. E. (2007). Disability, race/ethnicity and gender: Themes of cultural oppression, acts of individual resistance. *American Journal of Community Psychology, 39*, 145–161.

Miller, E. (2004). Gay, lesbian, and bisexual individuals with SCI. *SCI Psychosocial Process, 17*(2), 126–128.

Miller, E. (2005). SCI among Asian Americans: Counseling implications. *SCI Psychosocial Process, 18*(3), 196–198.

Nosek, M. A., Howland, C. A., Rintala, D. H., Young, M. E., & Chanpong, G. F. (2001). National study of women with physical disabilities: Final report. *Sexuality & Disability, 19*(1), 5–39.

Rahman, R. O., Albright, K. J., & Yaroslavsky, I. (2005). Perceived stress and life satisfaction in women with a spinal cord injury: An exploratory look at racial differences. *SCI Psychosocial Process, 18*(10), 4–8.

Renner, W., & Berry, J. W. (2011). The ineffectiveness of group interventions for female Turkish migrants with recurrent depression. *Social Behavior and Personality, 39*(9), 1217–1234.

Saetermoe, C. L., Dorothy Scattone, D., & Kim, K. H. (2001). Ethnicity and the stigma of disabilities. *Psychology and Health, 16*, 699–713.

Salazar, C. F. (2006). Conceptualizing multiple identities and multiple oppressions in clients' lives. *Counseling and Human Development, 39*(1), 1–18.

Sevak, P., Houtenville, A. J., Brucker, D. L., & O'Neill, J. (2015). Individual characteristics and the disability employment gap. *Journal of Disability Policy Studies, 26*(2), 80–88.

Simpson, R. A., & Salsgiver, R. O. (2005). An ethnoconscious approach to working with African Americans with disabilities. *SCI Psychosocial Process, 18*(3), 150–157.

Smart, J. F., & Smart, D. W. (1997). The racial-ethnic demography of disability. *Journal of Rehabilitation, 63*(4), 9–15.

Thurston, W. E., Coupal, S., Jones, C. A., Crowshoe, L. F. J., Marshall, D. A., Hornik, J., & Barnable, C. (2014). Discordant indigenous and provider frames explain challenges in improving access to arthritis care: A qualitative study using constructivist grounded theory. *International Journal of Equity in Health, 13*, 46–63.

Tremain, S. (2000). Queering disabled sexuality studies. *Sexuality & Disability, 18*(4), 291–299.

Zincir, H., Özkan, F., Erten, K., & Ümit Sevig, E. (2011). Sexual lives and family function of women with family member with disability: Educational status and income level. *Sexuality & Disability, 29*, 197–206.

Handout 9.5a: Possible Topics

Disability and

African American

Chinese/Chinese American

Japanese/Japanese American

Asian/Asian American (specific country)

Middle Eastern (specific country)

American Indigenous

Pacific Islander

Latinx (specific heritage)

Gay male

Lesbian

Female

Gender nonconforming

Amish

Orthodox Jew

Muslim

Catholic

____

Handout 9.5b: Instructions for Students

The goal of your research into intersectionality is to inform clinical work with clients who inhabit more than one marginalized population. Research the intersectionality of disability and the other variable you selected or were assigned. Note which articles are empirical. Prepare a PowerPoint presentation of about 20 minutes (approximately 20 slides) on your research. Remember that you are covering *intersectionality*, not each topic separately.

Include

1. Any statistics on the number of people in the United States who fall into your chosen population.
2. Some insight into the amount of empirical and clinical literature there is on this population.
3. Key findings from the literature.
4. A brief YouTube or other video by a person with this intersectionality talking about their lived experience (or a vignette if no video could be found).
5. Clinical implications.

10 Immersion and Activism

SEVEN ACTIVITIES ARE included in this chapter. All have the goal of immersing participants in disability culture and lives and to convey a sense of the lived experiences of people with disabilities. The first two activities immerse them in the necessity of managing fatigue. The third activity makes them outsiders among a group of people with disabilities. The fourth activity focuses on a microaggressions. In the fifth activity, they experience what media would be like without sound, relying only on captioning. The sixth activity is about taking action in some way to further the integration of and ease the burdens for disabled people. For the last activity, which has to be done over a period of at least 4 weeks, participants respond to clinical vignettes, turning knowledge into skills.

Teaching Disability. Rhoda Olkin, Oxford University Press. © Oxford University Press 2021.
DOI: 10.1093/oso/9780190850661.003.0010

Activity 10.1: Pennies to Spend—Understanding Fatigue

Activity: Students have a finite number of pennies, each penny representing a unit of energy. Students may have a different number of pennies, depending on which disability they have been assigned. They must "spend" their allotted number of pennies going about their week without running out of pennies before the week is over.

Where: All the places a student goes during the week.

Purpose: Fatigue is a common symptom of many disabilities. However, fatigue is not the same as being tired, wherein a good night's sleep can resolve the problem. Disability fatigue is more akin to what one feels with the flu, where motion and actions and activities seem to take more energy than usual. The fatigue waxes and wanes and is related to the number and types of activities, food consumption, sleep, rest or exertion, pain, use of assistive devices, and myriad other factors. In this activity, pennies are the proxy for fatigue, and each student has a limited number of pennies to use throughout the week. Most activities do "cost" some number of pennies (as seen on Handout 10.1c). Some activities, such as rest or yoga, restore energy and thus increase the number of pennies available.

Learning Objectives

1. Compile and track data on each day's activities and the pennies earned and spent.
2. Create a plan to conserve and/or restore pennies.
3. Revise plans according to the number of pennies left.
4. Analyze the week's activities in light of fatigue factors as demonstrated by the number of pennies spent and remaining.
5. Write a synopsis of the experience over the week.

Materials: Handouts for teacher and for students.

Preparation: This activity takes more planning and explanation than some others but is not difficult to assign. (a) Students should be randomly assigned a disability, if they have not been already. (*See* Handout 6.4a *for a list of possible disabilities. Note that no student should be assigned his or her own disability.*) (b) The instructor should use the list of disabilities to assign pennies (which represent energy) to the disability that would require the most and the least energy. This gives an anchor at each end of the spectrum. (c) The students should separately assign a number of pennies to each disability. The average of those numbers becomes the number of pennies for that disability. For example, if three students give blindness 120, 190, and 210 pennies, the average rounds to 173, and that would be the number of pennies assigned to blindness. (*Note: You may choose to skip Steps b and c and use the pennies assigned in the teacher's handout.*) (d) Students can use Handout 10.1e on paper or online to track each day's activities and the number of pennies spent or earned. This tracking will be turned in.

Time: One full week.

Possible Outcomes: There tend to be four common outcomes. (a) Some students run out of pennies several days in and abandon the assignment. (b) Some students take the assignment so seriously that they cancel events (even calling in sick to work) when they are close to being out of pennies. (c) Students with children living at home tend to find there simply are not enough points to get through the week. (d) Some students with existing disabilities often say this activity is life changing and leads them to reevaluate their general level of activities and priorities.

Talking Points: This activity shows students one of the hidden aspects of disability, namely, fatigue management. However, the assignment can backfire if it results in increased pity for people with disabilities. Some students may notice that they had to use points needlessly because their disability was not accommodated in some way. This observation shifts the focus from pity to the ways in which the world disadvantages people with disabilities. Another point that might get raised is the possibility that people with disabilities should get some compensatory "perks," such as being able to drive in the carpool lane. This is an important discussion, as it raises the issue of distributive justice, whereby some people have to give up something (e.g., faster traffic) to make it easier for other people (e.g., more people in the carpool lane). Other discussion can focus on the different reactions students had to the activity; why some students gave up; the effects of having children; how choices were made about what activities to do or not do; how much energy basic tasks of living take (e.g., laundry, cooking, dishes); the advantages of mail order; and the added expenses of hiring assistance or using online services (e.g., for groceries).

Another aspect to address is insider/outsider differences. The major concerns of people with disabilities tend to be the social and interpersonal aspects of disability, while those without disabilities believe the hardest parts to be the limitations imposed by the condition. This activity focuses on the physical, which is one reason it can possibly backfire and arouse pity. However, when students have to make choices about what can and cannot be accomplished given their limited pennies to spend, often there are psychosocial consequences. For example, if you do not have the energy to plant the tomato plants you bought 2 days ago, what are the options available? Thus, a physical issue—not enough energy—becomes an interpersonal issue (getting someone to do it for you) or a financial issue (hiring someone to plant for you) or a loss (the tomatoes do not get planted and die). Energy management is a constant decision-making process because deciding to do one thing means not being able to do something else.

Grading Rubric: 1 point for each day tracked and 3 points for clarity of tracking system (10 points); 5 points for revision of plans to accommodate number of pennies; 10 points for a one-page synopsis of the experience and what was learned. Total: 25 points.

Additional Reading

Benedict, R. H. B., Wahlig, E., Bakshi, R., Fishman, I., Munschauer, F., Zivadinov, R., & Weinstock-Guttman, B. (2005). Predicting quality of life in multiple sclerosis: Accounting for physical disability, fatigue, cognition, mood disorder, personality, and behavior change. *Journal of the Neurological Sciences, 231*(1–2), 29–34. https://doi.org/10.1016/j.jns.2004.12.009

Gong, G., & Mao, J. (2016). Health-related quality of life among Chinese patients with rheumatoid arthritis: The predictive roles of fatigue, functional disability, self-efficacy, and social support. *Nursing Research, 65*(1), 55–67. https://doi.org/10.1097/NNR.0000000000000137

Motl, R. W., McAuley, E., Snook, E. M., & Gliottoni, R. (2006). Physical activity and quality of life in multiple sclerosis: Intermediary roles of disability, fatigue, mood, pain, self-efficacy and social support. *Journal of Psychology, Health and Medicine, 28*(18), 111–124. https://doi.org/10.1080/13548500802241902

Raina, K. D., Morse, J. Q., Chisholm, D., Leibold, M. L., Shen, J., & Whyte, E. (2016). Feasibility of a cognitive behavioral intervention to manage fatigue in individuals with traumatic brain injury. *Journal of Head Trauma Rehabilitation, 31*(5), e41–e49. https://doi.org/10.1097/HTR.0000000000000196

Riehm, K. E., Kwakkenbos, L., Carrier, M., Bartlett, S. J., Malcarne, V. L., Mouthon, L., . . . Scleroderma Patient-Centered Intervention Network Investigators. (2016). Validation of the Self-Efficacy for Managing Chronic Disease Scale: A scleroderma patient-centered intervention network cohort study. *Arthritis Care and Research, 68*(8), 1195–1200. https://doi.org/10.1002/acr.22807

Twigg, S., Hensor, E. M. A., Emery, P., Morgan, A. W., & Tennant, A. The relationship between disease activity and disability is mediated by pain and fatigue in early rheumatoid arthritis. *Annals of the Rheumatic Diseases, 76*(Suppl. 2), 227.

Yazici, G., Irkec, C., Guclu-Gunduz, A., Ozkul, C., Ozkan, T., Aydin, Y., . . . Nazliel, B. (2015). The effects of fatigue on functioning and quality of life in patients with multiple sclerosis. *Journal of the Neurological Sciences, 357*(Supplement 1), e353–354. https://doi.org/10.1016/j.jns.2015.08.1262

Handout 10.1a: Teacher Copy

Steps

1. Assign each student a disability (if not done for a previous exercise).
2. Have them research that disability (can be at home or in class) and in class or via PowerPoint teach it to the other students (if not done for a previous exercise).
3. Distribute Handout 10.1f, Student Copy, that explains the purpose of this activity.
4. Distribute Handout 10.1b with only *1 Low vision 325 pennies* and *15 Amyotrophic Lateral Sclerosis 125 pennie*s filled in. This gives the anchors for the energy (pennies) scale. In class, ask students to give an energy rating for each disability and then take the average rating across students, that is, the number of energy points for that disability to be entered into the table in Handout 10.1b. Alternatively, use the points system already in Handout 10.1b, which was developed using student ratings from three classes.
5. Distribute and review Handouts 10.1c and 10.1d with the class to make sure everyone understands how energy points (pennies) are used and gained. This is a time to have students add more items; they also can add their own items to the table.
6. Review Handout 10.1e to make sure students understand how to track their activities and pennies for the week.

Handout 10.1b: Energy Point System (i.e., Pennies per Week per Disability)

Rank	Disability	Pennies Allotted per Week
1	Low vision	325
2	Asperger syndrome	293
3	Diabetes type 1	283
4	Bipolar	268
5	Traumatic brain injury with post-traumatic stress disorder	233
6	Spinal cord injury, L1	231
7	Muscular dystrophy	222
8	Lupus	217
9	Polio/postpolio syndrome	215
10	Multiple sclerosis	206
11	Juvenile rheumatoid arthritis	205
12	Spina bifida	196
13	Cerebral palsy	196
14	Spinal cord injury, C4	159
15	Amyotrophic lateral sclerosis	125

Handout 10.1c: Energy Point System (Pennies) per Activity

Activity	Energy Points (Number of Pennies) Used
Going to work or school for 6–8 hours	25 pennies
Taking public transportation	15 pennies
Going out to dinner	10 pennies
Going out to breakfast or lunch	7 pennies
Doing homework	5 pennies/hour
Staying up late	6 pennies
Laundry	8 pennies
Commuting more than 15 minutes	1 penny/every 10 minutes > 15 minutes
Taking care of children 5 years old or younger	10 pennies/hour
Taking care of children 6–12 years old	5 pennies/hour
Taking care of children 13–18 years old	2 pennies/hour
Making the bed	3 pennies
Washing dishes from cooking and dinner	4 points
Cooking dinner	5 points
Other (student to fill in): __________ __________ __________ __________ __________ __________ __________ __________	

Handout 10.1d: Energy Points (Pennies) Earned

Activity	**Energy Points (Pennies) Gained**
30–45 minutes of rest or nap	+ 5 pennies
90 minutes of rest or nap	+ 7 pennies
Nighttime sleeping	+ 3 pennies/hour
Light exercise for 20 minutes (e.g., walking, lifting 3-pound weights, stretching)	+ 4 pennies
Yoga 1 hour or less	+ 3 pennies
Meditation or mindfulness 10 minutes or longer	+ 5 points

Handout 10.1e: Tracking System

Disability: ____________________ **Number of Pennies to Start:** ___________

Day	Activity	Number of Pennies Used	Number of Pennies Gained	Remaining Number of Pennies

Handout 10.1f: Student Copy

- In this module we are exploring the ways in which various disability factors might affect a person in day-to-day life. One of the key ways that disability affects functioning is through pain, fatigue, and/or weakness, factors that influence the amount of energy someone has.
- You have been assigned a disability. Each disability has a given number of "energy points." This week you have "pennies to spend," that is, a certain number of disability energy points that you can use during a 1-week period.
- Look up your disability to see how many points you have. For example, if you have muscular dystrophy, you have 222 points/week; the person with cerebral palsy has 196 points/week.
- When you are out of points, you have to rest or do some other activity to gain energy points (e.g., nap, yoga, meditation, mindfulness) until you can gain more points.
- *Keep a diary for 1 week* from today to the day before class. Note each day how many points you have used and on what activities and then how many points you have left for the week.
- Modify your activities as you can to conserve points.
- After the week is done, *write* what you have experienced and learned about being a person with a specific disability (1 page).
- *Turn in your diary and your 1 page on what you experienced and have learned from this activity.*

Activity 10.2: Making Choices—Managing Fatigue

Activity: Managing fatigue due to a chronic condition or disability involves making choices. Every choice to partake in an activity means making a choice about what to cut from one's schedule. This activity involves making choices.

Where: At home during the week.

Purpose: To illustrate that fatigue management means making choices, some of which are easier, some harder, and some that go to the core of self-definition.

Learning Objectives

1. List all of your activities for the week (e.g., each class, commuting, work, homework) as well as the number of clients, group sessions, or testing reports you do in 1 week.
2. Review and revise the list to include daily or weekly tasks such as toileting (e.g., showering, brushing teeth); dressing and putting away clothes; household tasks (e.g., laundry, changing sheets, grocery shopping, washing dishes, emptying the dish drainer or dishwasher); hobbies (e.g., knitting, gardening, hiking); include pet care if applicable. Add 3 points for every drink of alcohol and 1 point per cigarette smoked.
3. Assign every household task 2 points, every activity outside the house 5 points, and every client, group, or testing hour 5 points/hour.
4. Total your points for the week (e.g., 125), then subtract 20% because of disability-related fatigue (e.g., 125 - 25 = 100).
5. Revise your list of activities to use only the smaller number of points, that is, reduce your activities by 20%.
6. For 1 week, actually do only the items that are on the revised list.

Materials: Handouts 10.2a (Example), 10.2b (Instructions for Students), and 10.2c (Possible Additional Activities).

Preparation: After explaining the activity to students, it is helpful to go over the example in Handout 10.2a in class before students do the activity on their own.

Time: 3 hours.

Possible Outcomes: Students quickly learn to shave points by using online services for grocery delivery and hiring people to do tasks. But if this doesn't shave off enough points (and it usually won't), they then have to make decisions to cut out some activities. Once the required activities are given points, it is usually recreational activities that have to be cut.

Talking Points: (a) Alcohol and cigarette use is costly in terms of fatigue. (b) People rarely mind giving up household tasks, but it is harder to give up recreational activities. (c) Giving up too many leisure and recreational activities can lead to decreased socialization and even isolation, which are risk factors for depression; depression then increases feelings of fatigue. (d) Hiring people to do things for you or to use delivery services costs money. There is always a trade-off between time/energy and money.

Grading Rubric: 15 points total: 5 points for Learning Objectives 1, 2, and 3; Learning Objectives 4 and 5 earn 4 points; 6 points for Learning Objective 6.

Additional Reading

Asano, M., & Finlayson, M. L. (2014). Meta-analysis of three different types of fatigue management interventions for people with multiple sclerosis: Exercise, education and medication. *Multiple Sclerosis International, 2014*, 1–12. https://doi.org/10.1155/2014/798285

Burns, T. (2018). Estimating and managing fatigue for our patients: Are we measuring up? *Muscle & Nerve, 58*(2), 197–203. https://doi.org/10.1002/mus.26125

Cincotta, M. C., Engelhard, M. M., Stankey, M., & Goldman, M. (2016). Fatigue and fluid hydration status in multiple sclerosis: A hypothesis. *Multiple Sclerosis Journal, 22*(11), 1438–1443.

Corwin, E. J., Klein, L. C., & Rickelman, K. (2002). Predictors of fatigue in healthy young adults: Moderating effects of cigarette smoking and gender. *Biological Research for Nursing, 3*(4), 222–233.

Hickman, J. S., Hanowski, R. J., Price, J., & Mabry, J. E. (2018). 10 International conference on managing fatigue: Managing fatigue to improve safety, wellness, and effectiveness. *Accident Analysis and Prevention, 117*, 1–2. https://doi.org/10.1016/j.aap.2018.05.012

Jensen, M. P., Alschuler, K. N., Smith, A. E., Verrall, A. M., Goetz, M. C., & Molton, I. R. (2011). Pain and fatigue in persons with postpolio syndrome: Independent effects on functioning. *Physical Medicine and Rehabilitation, 92*(11), 1796–1801.

Lovas, J., Tran, Y., Middleton, J., Bartrop, R., Moore, N., & Craig, A. (2016). Managing pain and fatigue in people with spinal cord injury: A randomized controlled trial feasibility study examining the efficacy of massage therapy. *Spinal Cord, 55*, 162–166.

Van den Akker, L. E., Beckerman, H., Collette, E. H., Eijssen, I. C. J. M., Dekker, J., & de Groot, V. (2016). Effectiveness of cognitive behavioral therapy for the treatment of fatigue in patients with multiple sclerosis: A systematic review and meta-analysis. *Journal of Psychosomatic Research, 90*, 33–42. https://doi.org/10.1016/j.jpsychores.2016.09.002

Handout 10.2a: Example

Weekly Activity	Points per Activity	Total Points
Study group, 2 hours	5	10
Practicum: 4 clients	5	20
Three classes, 3 hours each	5	15
Commuting, 6 trips	5	30
Laundry	2	2
Walking dog daily, 7 days	2	14
Friday night social hour	5	5
Two drinks Friday night	3	6
Grocery shopping	5	5
Getting dressed daily	2	14
Getting undressed and putting away clothes daily	2	14
Brushing teeth twice daily	4	28
Washing dishes four times	2	8
Showering four times	2	8
Hiking with partner on Sunday	5	5
Taking out garbage three times	2	6
ACTUAL TOTAL WEEKLY POINTS: 190 GOAL: TOTAL WEEKLY POINTS REDUCED BY 20%: 152		

Handout 10.2b: Instructions for Students

1. Review the example (Handout 10.2a) in class with peers and instructor and make sure you understand what to do.
2. List *all* of your activities for the week (e.g., each class, commuting, work, homework), as well as the number of clients, group sessions, or testing reports you do in 1 week.
3. Review and revise the list to include daily or weekly tasks such as toileting (e.g., showering, brushing teeth); dressing and putting away clothes; household tasks (e.g., laundry, changing sheets, grocery shopping, washing dishes, emptying the dish drainer or dishwasher); hobbies (e.g., knitting, gardening, hiking); include pet care, if applicable.
4. Assign every household task 2 points; every activity outside the house 5 points; and every client, group, or testing hour 5 points/hour (e.g., two clients equals 10 points). Add 3 points for every drink of alcohol and 1 point per cigarette smoked.
5. Total your points for the week (e.g., 125), then subtract 20% (e.g., 125 - 25 = 100).
6. Revise your list of activities to use only the smaller number of points, that is, reduce your activities by 20%.
7. *For 1 week*, actually do *only* the items that are on the revised list.
8. Keep a record of your activities and points.
9. Write a half-page on your learning and responses to this activity.

Handout 10.2c: Possible Additional Activities

A. Extend the time to do this assignment to 1 month; that is, for 1 month students are restricted to the smaller number of points. This is particularly recommended for students in rehabilitation counseling or psychology. It is a more accurate experience of managing fatigue over a longer period and how 1 week affects the next.

B. If the assignment is done for 1 week, add a second week where points have to be reduced by an additional 10%.

Activity 10.3: Outside in: Attending a Disability Event

Activity: Attend an event designed for (or that attracts) a sizable number of people with disabilities.

Where: Various locations in the greater community where the student lives.

Purpose: Often, people with apparent disabilities are quite conspicuous at public events attended primarily by able-bodied people. This activity reverses this asymmetry so that an apparently able-bodied person is the exception, and people with various disabilities are in abundance because the event is designed for them.

Learning Objectives

1. Discover ways to locate disability-focused events.
2. Experience being an outsider in a group of insiders.
3. Notice what features make an event universally accessible.

Materials: Notebook or phone to record notes.

Preparation: None required, though students may need help in class locating disability events (see Handout 10.3a for ideas; it would be useful to do this together in class and students might want to go in pairs to an event, but not more than pairs since the idea is to be an outsider).

Time: Several hours to a full day.

Possible Outcomes: Nondisabled students may find this eye-opening, but some may experience social awkwardness or even fright when not knowing how to behave in a context where disability is normative. Some may insist it was "just like any other group that's different," but they may be downplaying the differences and the effects of disabilities. Students of color especially may notice the ethnic composition of the group or may notice that there were more mixed-race couples with disabilities.

Talking Points: (a) How hard or easy was it to find an event to attend? (b) Notice how many wheelchairs at one event can make an event seem very crowded. (c) There might have been a hierarchy in who gets to sit where, in who gets helped, who goes first in a line, who gets out of the way for the other person; was anything noticeable? (d) Depending on the event, it might have been predominantly one ethnic group (often White); was this the case? (e) People with physical disabilities often move aggressively in a crowd as they are used to having to make their way through people; did you see evidence of this? (f) Did you notice any "disability norms," things that lots of people did that you wouldn't see at an event not geared toward disability (e.g., someone on crutches carrying things in their teeth; more offers of "Can I get that for you"?)

Grading Rubric: There can be a grade of 10 points just for going to the event, but if desired there can be points for writing a one-page report on the experience. If doing a report, it should address the points in Handout 10.3b (5 questions for 2 points each).

Additional Reading

Mik-Meyer, N. (2016). Disability, sameness, and equality: Able-bodied managers and employees discussing diversity in a Scandinavian context. *Scandinavian Journal of Disability Research*, *19*(2), 129–139. https://doi.org/10.1080/15017419.2016.1224201

Singer, J. (2020). Able-bodied fragility. *Digital Philology: A Journal of Medieval Cultures*, 9(1), 47–68.

Tchetchik, A., Eichhorn, V., & Biran, A. (2018). "Not on my vacation": Service encounters between able-bodied and disabled consumers—The case of high-contact service. *Journal of Policy Research in Tourism, Leisure and Events*, *10*(3), 204–220.

Handout 10.3a: Finding Disability Events

Search for the following on the Internet:

a. Disability events (this weekend) in my town)
b. Comedians with Disabilities Act
c. Ticket to Work (jobs for people with disabilities receiving Supplemental Security Income [SSI] or Social Security Disability Insurance [SSDI])
d. Disability Business Alliance
e. DiversABILITY
f. Abilities Expo Event (held in four locations yearly in October)
g. Documentary or film showings about disability
h. Wheelchair events
i. Sins Invalid (a disability justice performance group)
j. Autism Society
k. ADA National Network
l. gov.ca.gov/accessibility (substitute the abbreviation for your state instead of ca)
m. Lighthouse for the Blind and Visually Impaired
n. Disability rights (name of your state)

Call the following:

The local independent living center (ILC, or sometimes center for independent living)

Handout 10.3b: Points to Address in Your Report

1. What was the event? Who were the sponsors? How long did you stay?
2. Approximately how many people attended during the time you were there and about what percentage of them had visible disabilities?
3. What disability accommodations were noticeable (e.g., parking, entrances, signage, interpreters, captioning, seating arrangements, large print, people there to help)?
4. What did it feel like to be at the event?
5. As you thought about the event, what effect do you believe this experience had on you, if any?

Activity 10.4: Asking About Microaggressions

Activity: This is a small-group activity to ask questions of people with disabilities about their experiences of microaggressions. Students will work individually and then pool their information in small groups of four students. Each student has 1 week to ask 10 people with visible or invisible disabilities about the microaggressions they have encountered. After briefly explaining what a microaggression is, each student has a slightly different question to ask: What was the (a) worst one, (b) most recent one, (c) most common one, (d) most bothersome one?

Where: Practice and discussion in class, activity outside of class in the community.

Purpose: Disability exercises often incorporate putative simulations of the physical aspects of disability, but as discussed in Chapter 2, I am not recommending this approach. Instead, this activity focuses on learning what it is like to have a disability when interacting with the (mostly able-bodied) world.

Learning Objectives

1. Greater understanding of sources and types of ableist microaggressions.
2. Increasing emphasis on the social interaction experiences of people with disabilities and decreasing emphasis on the functional impairments.
3. Ability to integrate multiple sources of data.

Materials: Clipboard with data-keeping sheet on it, small slips of paper containing definition of microaggressions to hand to interviewees.

Preparation: Class discussion of what constitutes a microaggression and sharing of examples based on race/ethnicity, sexual orientation, gender identity, religion, disability, or other minority status or membership in a disadvantaged group. Included in the discussion should be the heightened emotions that often accompany the experience of a microaggression. Students should practice in class how to approach strangers with disabilities with a query about microaggressions.

Time: At least 1 hour in class for discussion and examples of microaggressions and to practice asking about microaggressions; 1 week for data collection; at least 1 hour of class time for students to pool data in small groups and then discuss with the entire class.

Possible Outcomes: Some students may contact the instructor and swear they couldn't locate anyone with a disability. Remind them that disability affects about 18% of the population, and 50% of all families; offer suggestions of good locations (near handicapped parking; near a center for independent living). Shyer students may find it easier to work in teams of two (which is acceptable if approved by the instructor). Still, whenever an activity involves contact and cooperation from people in the community, the outcomes are less predictable. Both process and content should be noted. Once there is a list of microaggressions from the shared data across the class, comparisons can be made to other groups that experience prejudice: Which microaggressions are similar, and which are unique to disability?

Talking Points: Note that intent behind the microaggressive statement or act is not the determinant of whether something is experienced as a microaggression. Generate several kinds of statements aggressors might say to try to neutralize the microaggression (e.g., "I was only kidding"). Also discuss the process: How easy or hard was it to locate people with disabilities in the community? How did they respond to being asked to volunteer to answer questions? Did asking strangers with disabilities cross some social boundaries for students? Were there types of disabilities they avoided, and why?

Grading Rubric: 10 points for individual lists (1 point per interview); 5 points for the small-group list and class discussion.

Additional Reading

Bogart, K., & Dunn, D. (2019). Ableism: Special issue introduction. *Journal of Social Issues: Special Issue: Ableism, 75*(3), 650–664. https://doi.org/10.1111/josi.12354

Kattari, S. K., Olzman, M., & Hanna, M. D. (2018). "You look fine!" Ableist experiences of people with invisible disabilities. *Affilia: Journal of Women and Social Work, 33*(4), 477–492. https://doi.org/10.1177/0886109918778073

Keller, R., & Galgay, C. E. (2010). Microaggressive experiences of people with disabilities. In D. W. Sue (Ed.), *Microaggressions and marginality: Manifestations, dynamics and impact* (pp. 241–267. Hoboken, NJ: Wiley.

Nario-Redmond, M. R. (2019). Introduction: Defining ableism. In *Ableism: The causes and consequences of disability prejudice* (pp. 1–32). Hoboken, NJ: Wiley.

Olkin, R., Hayward, H., Schaff Abbene, M., & VanHeel, G. (2019). The experiences of microaggressions against women with visible and invisible disabilities. *Journal of Social Issues: Special Issue: Ableism, 75*(3), 757–785.

Penwell Barnett, J. (2017). Intersectional harassment and deviant embodiment among Autistic adults: (Dis)ability, gender and sexuality. *Culture, Health & Sexuality, 19*(11), 1210–1224. https://doi.org/10.1080/13691058.2017.1309070

Sue, D. W. (2010). *Microaggressions in everyday life: Race, gender, and sexual orientation*. Hoboken, NJ: Wiley.

Williams, J. L. (2019). Disability as an intersectional diversity variable in the psychology curriculum. In J. A. Mena & K. Quina (Eds.), *Integrating multiculturalism and intersectionality into the psychology curriculum: Strategies for instructors* (pp. 157–168). Washington, DC: American Psychological Association.

Handout 10.4a: Definition of Microaggressions

Give the following to those interviewed.

"Everyday verbal, nonverbal, and environmental slights, snubs, or insults, whether intentional or unintentional, that communicate hostile, derogatory, or negative messages to target persons based solely upon their marginalized group membership" (Sue, 2010, p. 3).

Example: A nondisabled adult tells another adult who is experiencing disability-related fatigue: "All you need is a good night's sleep."

Example: A White male asks an Asian male from Sacramento, California: "Where are you really from?"

Handout 10.4b: Instructions to Students

For this activity, you are going to briefly interview 10 people with disabilities. At least five of these should be people you do not know, and up to five can be people you already know. For each person you interview, you will note their gender and ask the two questions below. Suggested script: "Excuse me, I'm conducting a survey about microaggressions experienced by people with disabilities. Could I have your permission to ask you two questions? This will take approximately 1 minute. I have a definition of microaggressions for you to read."

1. Can you tell me the (a) worst, (b) most recent, (c) most common, (d) most bothersome microaggression that you have experienced? (*Note:* Each small group of three to five people is to ask just one of these.)
2. Do you identify with any marginalized group (race/ethnicity, disability, religion, gender, sexual orientation, gender identity, national origin, any others)? Which one[s]?

Handout 10.4c: Survey Sheet

Person	Q1. Can you tell me the _____ microaggression that you have experienced?	Q2. Do you identify with any marginalized group?	Gender and Any Observations
P1			
P2			
P3			
P4			
P5			
P6			
P7			
P8			
P9			
P10			

Activity 10.5: What Deaf People Miss: Accessing Media Without Sound

Activity: Watching live and previously recorded television with and without sound on while also using close-captioning.

Where: At home.

Purpose: To compare oral and written versions of shows to aid understanding of accessibility for persons with hearing impairments or Deafhood.

Learning Objectives

1. To experience discrepancies in captioned and oral versions of live shows.
2. To chronicle the errors or omissions in captioned live and recorded shows.
3. To assess availability of sign language translation for live events on TV.

Materials: A television or computer with access to live and recorded TV shows.

Preparation: In class, students can work in small groups to design a table to record their observations. They can generate types of errors or omissions they believe they will observe, with space for other types. To get started, three common omissions are people's names or titles, swear words, and entire sentences.

Time: 2 hours of watching and recording results, 1 hour of writing results.

Possible Outcomes: Discussion postassignment should yield data showing frequent errors and omissions. Students/small groups can present their results, then compare across students/small groups. Results will differ for live events with sign language translation (which is generally more accurate) and for captioning of live shows. Recorded shows will have interesting discrepancies, such as slight changes to language and omission of swear words.

Talking Points: What specifically got changed or omitted? How important were these? Is there any rhyme or reason to the types of errors and omissions that are common? If you had to rely on captioning alone, what would you miss? What are the relative merits or drawbacks of using sign language versus captioning to follow a live show? What policy recommendations would you make to improve access?

Grading Rubric: 10 points total: 7 points for the presentation of results, based on thoroughness and clarity of results and depth of analysis; 3 points for specific policy recommendations.

Handout: A partial table to record results (Handout 10.5); students should add to the table.

Additional Reading

Berke, L., Caulfield, C., & Huenerfauth, M. (2017, October). Deaf and hard-of-hearing perspectives on imperfect automatic speech recognition for captioning one-on-one meetings. *Assets '17*, 155–164. https://dl.acm.org/doi/pdf/10.1145/3132525.3132541

Fresno, N. (2019). Of *bad hombres* and nasty women; the quality of the live close captioning in the 2016 U.S. final presidential debate. *Perspectives: Studies in Translation Theory and Practice, 27*(3), 350–366. https://doi.org/10.1080/0907676X.2018.1526960

Galvez, G. (2017, October 23–26). *Closed captioning and subtitling for social media.* Presented at SMPTE 2017 Annual Technical Conference and Exhibition, Los Angeles, CA. https://ieeexplore.ieee.org/abstract/document/8281436

Nam, S., & Fels, D. (2019). Simulation of subjective closed captioning quality assessment using prediction models. *International Journal of Semantic Computing, 13*(1), 45–65. https://doi.org/10.1142/S1793351X19400038

Rashid, R., Aitken, J., & Fels, D. (2006). Expressing emotions using animated text captions. In: K., Miesenberger, J., Klaus, W. L. Zagler, & A. I. Karshmer (Eds.), *Computers Helping People with Special Needs. ICCHP 2006. Lecture Notes in Computer Science, vol 4061*. Springer: Berlin, Heidelberg.

Sharma, D., & Rao, R. R. (2018). The combined effect of captioning and sign language in understanding television content in deaf. *Journal of Communication Disorders, Deaf Studies and Hearing Aids, 6*, 1–7. DOI: 0.4172/2375-4427.1000182.

Simpson, M. N., Barrett, J., Bell, P. J., & Renals, S. (2016, September 8–12). *Just-in-time prepared captioning for live transmissions.* Presented at IBC 2016 Conference, Amsterdam, Netherlands. https://doi.org/10.1049/ibc.2016.0027

Handout 10.5: Recording Observations

Show watched: ______________ **Live or Recorded:** L R **Time: Start:** ________________ **Stop:** ________________		
Findings	**Errors**	**Omissions**
Names		
Person's title or occupation		
Swear words		
Sentence omitted		
(*Students in small groups should add their own categories here; categories can be added while watching a show.*)		

Activity 10.6: Taking Action

Activity: Pick a problem encountered by people with disabilities that exists at the local or state level to research, interviewing users related to the problem, and writing to your mayor, city council, state representative, or governor about the problem, with data supporting the existence of the problem, a story that exemplifies the problem, and a proposed solution.

Where: At home.

Purpose: To understand the real-world consequences of a specific problem on end users (i.e., people with disabilities). To turn knowledge about a problem into an action with potential for resolution of the problem.

Learning Objectives

1. Identifying and researching a local-level problem.
2. Conducting interviews to get first-person accounts of the effects of the problem.
3. Developing possible solutions to the problem.
4. Communicating effectively with an elected official.

Materials: Internet to conduct literature search, recorder to tape interviews.

Preparation: Students may find it helpful to peruse the articles in Additional Reading to broaden their scope of problem areas affecting people with disabilities. Class time may be useful to discuss the readings and generate ideas for topics. Examples of problems: No gas station that pumps gas for those with handicapped placards or license plates; lack of curb cuts; stores that are inaccessible due to overstuffed aisles; restaurants without accessible bathrooms; ATM machines that are too high at checkout lines; lack of Braille signage for public places; no large-print versions of bus lines; city/town website that is incompatible with screen readers for the blind.

Time: Allow at least 3 weeks for completion of the assignment. Then one class period could be used to exchange and discuss findings.

Possible Outcomes: Students may need assistance with each part of the assignment: choosing a problem, gathering lived experiences, creating solutions, and knowing who to contact. Some may feel discouraged by how much work it takes for just one area of issues; others may feel empowered by the experience. It is hoped some students will become disability allies.

Talking Points: Persons with disabilities experience discrimination in almost all aspects of life, including employment, housing, transportation, leisure and entertainment events, politics, socialization, and more. Generally, court cases have used disability-specific laws in the arguments, rather than the broader Fourteenth Amendment to the Constitution. Thus, each issue gets fought separately and mostly through legal action. If a city or town wanted to make sweeping changes to ensure accessibility and inclusion in every venue and aspect of its municipality, what would it have to do to ensure success? How might people with disabilities be involved in such a project?

Grading Rubric: 15 points total: (a) choosing a specific and well-defined problem to work on, 2 points; (b) researching the problem and writing a one-page synopsis, 5 points; (c) gathering lived experiences from people with disabilities and opinions of experts, 5 points; (d) finding the elected official with power over the issue, and writing a letter to that person, with suggested solutions, 3 points. Additional points can be given for a presentation to class.

Handouts: 10.6a: (Instructions for Students) and 10.6b: (Some Possible Problems to Research).

Additional Reading

Altmann, N., & Kasper, E. T. (2019). *Judicial scrutiny and disability: How the Supreme Court applies the Fourteenth amendment to disability cases.* MINDS@UW Eau Claire. http://digital.library.wisc.edu/1793/80220

Corby, S., William, L., & Richard, S. (2018). Combatting disability discrimination: A comparative critique of France and Great Britain. *European Journal of Industrial Relations, 25*(1), 41–56. https://doi.org/10.1177/0959680118759169

Darcy, S., Taylor, T., & Green, J. (2016). "But I can do the job": Examining disability employment practice through human rights complaint cases. *Disability & Society, 31*(9), 1242–1274.

Goggin, G. (2011). Disability, mobiles, and social policy: New modes of communication and governance. In J. Katz (Ed.), *Mobile communication: Dimensions of social policy* (pp. 259–272). New Brunswick, NJ: Transaction.

Kett, M., Cole, E., & Turner, J. (2020). Disability, mobility and transport in low- and middle-income countries: A thematic review. *Sustainability, 12*(2), 589–607. https://doi.org/10.3390/su12020589

King, M., Shields, N., Imms, C., Black, M., & Ardern, C. (2013). Participation of children with intellectual disability compared with typically developing children. *Research in Developmental Disabilities, 34*, 1854–1862.

McMillen, R., & Alter, F. (2017). Social media, social inclusion, and museum disability access. *Museums and Social Issues.* http://dx.doi.org/10.1080/15596893.2017.1361689

McNaughton, D., & Light, J. (2013). The iPad and mobile technology revolution: Benefits and challenges for individuals who require augmentative and alternative communication. *Augmentative & Alternative Communication, 29*(2), 107–116. https://doi.org/10.3109/07434618.2013.784930

Morris, J., Mueller, J., Jones, M. L., & Lippincott, B. (2013). Wireless technology use and disability: Results from a national survey. *Journal of Technology and Persons with Disabilities, 1*(23), 70–80.

Murray, T. (2018). Disability discrimination in the workplace: When choice of jurisdiction matters. *The Proctor, 38*(2), 20.

Solish, A., Perry, A., & Minnes, P. (2010). Participation of children with and without disabilities in social, recreational, and leisure activities. *Journal of Applied Research in Intellectual Disabilities, 23*, 226–236.

Stanton-Chapman, T. L., & Schmidt, E. L. (2017). Creating an inclusive playground for children of *all* abilities: West Fork playground in Cincinnati, Ohio. *Children, Youth and Environments, 27*(3), 124–137.

Weber, M. C. (2017). Meaningful access and disability discrimination: The role of social science and other empirical evidence. *Cardoza Law Review, 39*(2), 650–668.

Handout 10.6a: Instructions for Students

You are going to take steps to make a change in the real world for people with disabilities in your community. There are 6 steps in this process:

1. Look over the suggested readings and think about one problem area that affects persons with disabilities in your community. Select one problem that is definable and specific for your focus.
2. Research the problem area you selected. Then write a one-page synopsis with a clear definition of the problem, discussing at least three articles that are relevant to this problem.
3. Gather information from persons with disabilities about their lived experiences related to this problem and from professionals who may have knowledge and opinions about the problem.
4. Identify the elected official who would be the best one to contact about this problem. It might be a local person (e.g., a council representative), a city leader (e.g., a mayor), an elected representative to your state legislature, or a state representative or senator to the U.S. Congress.
5. Write to your selected official with a clear statement of the problem area, one to two collected anecdotes from persons with disabilities or professionals, and a suggested solution to the problem.
6. Optional: Your instructor may ask you to give a presentation to the class.

Handout 10.6b: Some Possible Problems to Research

1. Is there sufficient handicapped parking for the needs of the community (e.g., at movie theaters, music venues, popular stores, city streets)?
2. Does the city have a map showing where handicapped parking exists and how many spots there are in each area?
3. Are there audible signals at crosswalks? How many, where, and should there be more?
4. Is all the public transportation easily accessed by persons with intellectual disabilities?
5. Are there sign language interpreters for all public meetings?
6. Does the city have a universal access park and play equipment for children with various disabilities?
7. Are important services (e.g., rehabilitation, physical therapy, most doctor's offices, dentists, police, Department of Motor Vehicles, post office) available by public transportation from all parts of town (including and especially the poorer parts of town).
8. Is city communication to residents available in large print?
9. Is there a local independent living center, how is it funded, and what services does it provide?
10. Are there licensed counselors or therapists trained in working with people with disabilities?
11. Is there a cap on the number of children with disabilities who can be identified by the school?
12. Do emergency plans adequately consider accessibility for all types of disabilities and the needs of people who may need to use electricity (to power medical devices) or bring a service animal?

Activity 10.7: Strengthening Clinical Skills: Responding to Vignettes

Activity: Addressing skills by reading clinical vignettes of clients with disabilities and thinking through emotional reactions, clinical issues, and specific verbal responses.

Where: In class as a discussion or at home as homework.

Purpose: To use attitudes and knowledge to promote culturally responsive clinical skills.

Learning Objectives

1. To increase awareness of one's own emotional reactions to specific disabled clients and their situations.
2. To become more comfortable addressing disability issues directly in therapy.
3. To consider alternate ways of responding to clients to create more choices of therapeutic responses.
4. To tolerate making mistakes in the service of learning.

Materials: Clinical vignettes with various clients with disabilities.

Preparation: No preparation is required that is specific to this activity, but doing this without any prior readings about disability is likely to be less effective.

Time: There are eight vignettes. If they are all done at once, there is no learning in between. I suggest doing one per week.

Possible Outcomes: It is important to help students link their own emotional responses and cognitions to what they want to do or say next. Students should be encouraged to give a response that is verbatim what they would say, or how they would think about the immediate and longer term goals, depending on the vignette. Initially, it can be helpful to slow the process down (e.g., "What do you feel in response to what you just read?" then "What initial thoughts come to your mind?") before students formulate a response.

Talking Points: What were your emotional responses to each vignette? What about some vignettes make them more difficult? How have your responses changed over time? How does intersectionality come into play in each vignette? What other cultural factors need to be considered? What language or specific words did you find you stumbled over? What was it like to be direct about disability? What steps might you take to further your comfort, knowledge, and skill levels?

Grading Rubric: (a) If done in class, no grading. (b) If done as homework, this should be graded bimodally: full points for completing the assignment (2 points/vignette), but no evaluation on the quality of the responses, to promote students' comfort in responding. (c) The vignettes could be used as a pre- and postassignment, before doing reading and some of the other activities in this book and after, to have students evaluate their own changes. That evaluation could be done in writing and graded (full points if completed and thoughtfully done).

Handout: 10.7: Eight Clinical Vignettes. These are currently in the order in which I've used them, and there is some slight increase in complexity over the eight. One vignette asks students to watch a YouTube video first. Vignette 8 has questions that require responses.

Additional Reading

Forber-Pratt, A. J., Mueller, C. O., & Andrews, E. E. (2019). Disability identity and allyship in rehabilitation psychology: Sit, stand, sign, and show up. *Rehabilitation Psychology, 64*(2), 119–129. https://doi.org/10.1037/rep0000256

McInnis, E. E. (2016). Critical literature review: Effectiveness of individual psychodynamic psychotherapy for adults with intellectual disabilities. *Advances in Mental Health and Intellectual Disabilities, 10*(4), 233–247. https://doi.org/10.1108/AMHID-09-2015-0040

Mona, L. R., Hayward, H., & Cameron, R. P. (2019). Cognitive behavior therapy and people with disabilities. In G. Y. Iwamasa & P. A. Hays (Eds.), *Culturally responsive cognitive behavior therapy: Practice and supervision* (pp. 257–285). Washington, DC: American Psychological Association. https://doi.org/10.1037/0000119-011

Olkin, R. (2006). Persons of color with disabilities. In M. Constantine (Ed.), *Clinical practice with people of color: A guide to becoming culturally competent* (pp. 162–182). New York: Teacher's College Press.

Olkin, R. (2008). Social warrior or unwitting bigot? *Professional Psychology: Research and Practice, 39*(5), 488–497.

Olkin, R. (2017). *Disability-affirmative therapy: A case formulation template for your clients with disabilities.* New York: Oxford University Press.

Olkin, R., & Taliaferro, G. (2005). Evidence-based practices have ignored people with disabilities: Dialogue. In J. Norcross, L. Beutler, & R. Levant (Eds.), *Evidence-based practices in mental health* (pp. 353–359, 365–367). Washington, DC: APA.

Handout 10.7: Eight Clinical Vignettes

1. Phil

Phil, a Latino lawyer in his late 30s, arrived for his first session in a manual wheelchair. He carried with him a transfer board—a smooth, flat, rectangular board about 1 by 2 feet—which he uses at work to help him slide from his wheelchair to his desk chair. However, the chairs in my office, as in most therapists' offices, are lower, cushiony, soft, designed to encourage sitting back, and swivel—all factors that made transferring to them more difficult. We spent about 10 minutes trying out different seating arrangements in the office. I encouraged this by stating something along the lines of "It's worth taking the time now, for you to be comfortable here." We ultimately found that my desk chair worked best for him, and prior to his future appointments I removed one "client" chair and replaced it with my desk chair. This gesture conveyed patience, acceptance, understanding, and a collaborative stance, more than words ever could. Nonetheless, a different client with similar transfer abilities may have been impatient with this process, just wanting to get on with the work of therapy. After all, the client is paying for the time.

2. Robert

Robert is an unemployed White man in his 30s, living alone in a one-bedroom apartment. He has paraplegia and uses an electric wheelchair and has limited use in both hands. Despite an undergraduate degree in journalism and 5 years of job experience as a stringer on a small newspaper, he has been unable to find a job for the past 4 years. His presenting problem is depression and loneliness. When the therapist suggests that there is nothing wrong with him that a job in journalism couldn't fix, he responds, "I don't want any of that victim crap."

3. Lori

Lori is a White married woman of 24 who comes from Oklahoma. She was referred for therapy by the doctor who treats her for ulcerative colitis (UC), who told her, "You need to work on your anxiety." She was an athlete in high school and college, and this is a big part of her identity. She currently is worried that she won't be able to continue playing or that she will let her teammates down. She was raised with the doctrine "no excuses" so she feels that her UC is an "excuse" for taking it easy on herself. Thus, it takes a severe level of symptoms for her to slow down. This led to her current situation where she is barely able to leave the house. She feels guilty that she is not working to help with household expenses, that she doesn't feel sexual, that she often cannot manage to cook dinner, and that she relies on her husband for reassurance and calming. Lori does not think of herself as "a woman with a disability" but as someone who has a chronic condition. She is only just beginning to maybe see a connection between her anxiety and stress and her UC symptoms. The feedback loop is not immediate, so her behavior and emotional state do not usually result in symptoms immediately. This makes it hard for her to "learn" about herself.

4. Caroline

Caroline is the married mother to an 11-year-old son, Nick, who has a genetic mutation (missing one chromosome), and a daughter age 8. She works in real estate, and her husband is an engineer. Nick's symptoms are similar to both attention deficit hyperactivity disorder and a learning disorder. He is clumsy, with poor gross and fine motor coordination. Notably he has difficulty learning from experience; for example, last year he insisted on going to the school picnic, but wanted to leave after 15 minutes, being overwhelmed at the number of people. Yet this year he insisted to his mother that they should go again. When she reminds him of the experience last year, he says, "Oh, yeah." But then the next day he will ask again about going. As he gets older, the distance between him and his peers gets larger, in terms of both his academics and his social behavior.

Caroline says that people often try to give her advice—send him to a special school, put him in a regular school, try a social skills group, get him a tutor, he needs therapy, playing an instrument would help his brain—and each time she thinks, "I'm not doing enough for him; there is more I could do for him." In the first session of therapy, she asks you who should be in therapy—her? Her and her husband? Her son? The whole family?

5. Michael

Michael is a Black gay man in his late 20s with muscular dystrophy (MD). He uses a respirator for about 8 hours a day and an electric wheelchair. A college graduate in engineering, he's unemployed, and the Department of Rehabilitation has been of limited assistance in helping him find employment (they tried to place him in a sheltered workshop). One friend from college lives nearby, but he's lost contact with other college friends and doesn't meet many people in his current state of joblessness.

Michael's mother lives in town, and he goes there for lunch or dinner twice a week and talks to her almost daily. He came out to his mother after his father died, and her initial reaction was "Another thing?!" (i.e., another stigmatized identity). However, she has come around to being quite accepting of him being gay.

His father died about 12 years ago; his mother remarried 3 years ago and is wanting more time with her husband. Although she never states this, she feels Michael is too dependent on her, and she doesn't want as much contact as they now have. But she feels guilty about this and unable to take any action on it unless she knows he has other people close to him. Michael also would like to expand his social network but is frustrated in doing so. He feels very comfortable with his mother, and others don't measure up in terms of their initial responses to his disability. Thus, the cycle of Michael's overreliance on her is continued by both of them.

Michael's model of disability combines elements of the moral model (he feels deep shame about his disability, avoids other people with disabilities); the medical model (he gets passive with doctors, and hopes for a cure for MD in his lifetime); and the social model (he was able to advocate for himself in college and is familiar with relevant laws and rights).

Michael's initial reason for seeking therapy is depression. He says he feels "bored" and "empty." He has had sexual encounters with anonymous men from "devotee"[1] websites, but never a romantic relationship, which he wants very much. Think about (a) your countertransference; (b) what you will have to do to be truly empathic with Michael; (c) what might be the entry point into therapy for him (i.e., where can you start the treatment?).

6. Celestia

Celestia is a 29-year-old woman who is enrolled in a graduate program in counseling psychology. She is fluent in American Sign Language (ASL) and speaks a little bit of English. Two ASL interpreters accompany her to all classes (they are required to switch every 20 minutes). The cost for these interpreters is higher than the tuition Celestia pays, something that she has been made well aware of. Also no one knows how to pronounce her name. When she was asked about it, she replied that she didn't care how it was pronounced since she couldn't hear it; she chose the name because she liked the way it looked on paper.

Problems arose when Celestia took an assessment course. The instructor did not want to let Celestia use a sign language interpreter to administer tests. He insisted that assessment is all about standardization, and it would invalidate the results if the administration was not standardized by having it in ASL and English. However, Celestia wanted to be able to do assessments with Deaf clients and requested that she be allowed to do this for the class assignments. The instructor declined, as there were issues with finding volunteers who were deaf and used sign language, and he was worried about liability. Additionally, he was unaware

1 Before responding to the vignette, you need to watch the assigned video on devotees at https://www.youtube.com/watch?v=9FAhMbtqcNo. (*Note*: The video says it is 44 minutes long, but it repeats, starting at about 25 minutes.)

of the problems of using English-based assessments with deaf clients: Were the norms valid? Were the same underlying constructs being assessed? He did do some research and found that there were some studies on using the Beck Depression Inventory and the Minnesota Multiphasic Personality Inventory (MMPIo with deaf clients, but not much else.

In her second semester of graduate school, Celestia considered dropping out. She was lonely (the interpreters could only interpret for classes or official functions, but not for time between events, so Celestia could not interact with her peers). She missed lots of information since students shared information verbally, so she was behind in applying for a practicum. She was overwhelmed by the amount of reading since English was not her first language (ASL was). She was discouraged by her assessment course instructor, feeling he didn't think she would pass the course and his unwillingness to make what she felt were reasonable accommodations. She thought about filing a grievance but didn't know her options and also didn't want to draw even more attention to herself. Also she didn't know if her grievance would be successful—maybe it was accurate that if she couldn't administer assessments she shouldn't be in this field.

It was at this point that Celestia sought therapy. She did not want a deaf therapist as the Deaf community is fairly insular, that is, lots of people within the community know each other or of each other. So she sought out a hearing therapist (YOU) with some competence with disability (even though Celestia does not identify deafness as a disability, she understands that this is her milieu politically).

There are logistical issues that have to be handled quickly for you to be able to see Celestia. These include hiring interpreters (One? Two? From where?), making sure your intake forms are deaf friendly, discussing confidentiality, deciding on fees (are you allowed to ask the client to pay for the interpreters?). These things feel so overwhelming to you that you become "deskilled," that is, forget your basic therapist skills as you struggle with basic communication needs.

But, imagine that the Department of Vocational Rehabilitation will pay for the interpreters. Celestia can afford your reduced fee. You go over the intake forms with her in the first session instead of asking her to fill them out in advance. You ascertain that the main presenting problem is Celestia's question of whether she should drop out of the program, though you suspect there are many psychosocial issues contained in that question.

Think through:

Your countertransference.

Celestia's probable relationship with you both initially and over time—how you might foster a positive therapeutic alliance.

What research you might have to do on your own.
What behaviors of your own that you might need to keep an eye on in sessions.
What other issues might Celestia be facing.
Possible resources that you might enlist.

7. Ruby

Ruby is an African American woman in her 40s. She works at a bank as a loan officer. In the first session, she tells you straight off: "I wanted to let you know that I have multiple sclerosis, which is a neurological disorder. Sometimes I have a few weeks where it affects me more and other times it affects me very little. You may notice I walk a bit slower. Oh, also I have trouble with my memory. If my phone beeps it is to remind me to do something. And if you think I'm not paying attention, would you say my name and remind me to pay attention? Any questions?"

And now you, the therapist, say . . . ???

8. Carl

Carl is a 44-year-old, White, heterosexual male. He is married with two children and is well respected as a manager in a large company. Until 9 months ago, Carl was healthy and fit, a happy childhood.

Carl began to experience low-level fatigue and digestive and elimination issues, which he largely tried to compensate for and ignore. After taking a prescription medication for an infection, his symptoms significantly increased to the point that he needed to take a medical leave from work. At the time he was seen in therapy, he was beginning to feel a little bit better as the side effects of the medication were cleared from his system, but still not good enough to return to work or eat without discomfort.

Because Carl had good insurance, financial stability, and lives in an urban area, he was able to consult with numerous respected healthcare specialists and spent months being tested, poked, and prodded. He also followed every referral, no matter how much he questioned the efficacy of the method, and had seen dozens of Western and complementary and alternative medicine practitioners. However, although many diagnoses were potentially ruled out, he still had no definitive diagnosis or lessening of his symptoms.

It is very unfortunate that once a specialist has ruled out her or his diagnostic area of expertise, there was usually no referral or other assistance. Carl was left to research his symptoms on the Internet, discovering potential diagnoses and finding referrals to practitioners with that area of expertise. Therefore, a good primary care physician (PCP) is imperative to coordinate and continue to follow the person, one who is skilled in managing complex medical issues requiring multiple practitioners, and Carl found a PCP he liked.

The PCP referred Carl for hypnosis for symptom mitigation. In the intake with you, the psychotherapist, he described himself as overwhelmed, depressed, and stressed and stated that he hoped to learn some stress management tools but wasn't optimistic that the therapy would impact his symptoms. He also said that he was a "typical Type A" and someone who didn't normally get depressed and was frustrated with his depression, his situation, and his doctors. He also said that he felt like a watered-down version of his former self. It was extremely difficult for him to adjust when he didn't know what he was adjusting to. Carl wondered if he should just try to accept his symptoms or keep seeing healthcare practitioners until somebody gave him some answers.

Questions on Carl

Describe your treatment goals and your plan for the first five sessions.

(Do not say that you will "build rapport"—that can be assumed, and you have to be doing something while rapport is being built.)

1. Two long-term goals: (2 points)
2. Three short-term goals on the way to long-term goals: (3 points)
3. Session 1: (2 points)
4. Session 2: (2 points)
5. Session 3: (2 points)
6. Session 4: (2 points)
7. Session 5: (2 points)

D Conclusions

THE FINAL CHAPTER is about how we can assess the effects of the activities in this book. It begins with some discussion about how we measure attitudes toward disability, as well as what it is we want to evaluate. A modified social distance scale for disability, based on the original from the 1920s by Bogardus used to assess prejudice towards Chinese Americans, is included; this would allow comparisons across classes and with published data. Acknowledging possible emotional reactions, whether positive or negative, to disabled persons is important in addressing those reactions, so a table of possible responses is included. An assessment of able-bodied privilege is useful to highlight those aspects of daily life that persons without disabilities take for granted. It can also be used when students are assigned a disability and they fill out the assessment as if they had that disability. I've included a brief quality of life measure I developed that my students have used in dissertations. Although very brief, it distills the key elements across many different extant quality of life measures. Also included is a brief knowledge quiz that could be used pre- and post-education (whether in class or through readings or activities). Lastly is a rating scale of attitudes and skills. Ultimately skills in better serving clients with disabilities is a critical goal, so some assessment of skills is important. I suggest that any assessments be conducted both in the short term after an activity or activities are completed, and if at all possible at longer follow up times. Previous literature suggests that short-term positive gains are either not maintained in the long term or are even reversed. Although many of the activities in this book have been used, at this point there are no long-term data about their effects. Note that references for the citations appear at the end of this chapter.

11 Assessing Outcomes

WE HAVE SEEN moments in American life when there has been a sea change in social norms. Examples include the #MeToo movement, Black Lives Matter in the aftermath of the death of George Floyd, and acceptance of gay marriage after the Supreme Court decision. Disability has not had its moment. The passage of the Rehabilitation Act (1973) and the Americans with Disabilities Act (1990) led to increased accessibility of public spaces but did not lead to the kind of shifts to hearts and minds we saw with other movements. Thus, it is not surprising that, as noted in Chapter 2, implicit bias toward disability has not decreased.

I do not pretend that the activities in this book will affect implicit bias. I would like that to happen, but without data I cannot say it will. What I do hope is that nothing herein will have an effect opposite to that which I intend, that is, to focus participants on the *physical difficulties* associated with disability, and not the environmental and interpersonal aspects. In so doing, it might elicit more pity or poorer attitudes. Some of the activities are designed to increase knowledge from an insider perspective, and many of the activities attempt to shift the focus from persons with disabilities themselves to the burdens imposed by an unjust society that discriminates against disabled people. We need data on how to best achieve these goals, and debriefing the activities is important, especially if there are undesired consequences. Ultimately, the goal is to increase cultural responsivity and skill levels for therapists working with their clients with disabilities. How can we know if we have done that?

Teaching Disability. Rhoda Olkin, Oxford University Press. © Oxford University Press 2021.
DOI: 10.1093/oso/9780190850661.003.0011

Attitudes and Beliefs. Factors that influence attitudes toward disability are information (knowledge) and beliefs (Yuker, 1994). Several of the activities focus on beliefs. For example, Activity 6.1 is about illness beliefs, and Activity 6.2 is about models of disabilities, that is, belief systems about disability.

There are several measures of attitudes toward disability, only a few of which are discussed. One of the most used is Yuker's Attitudes Towards Disability Scale (Yuker, 1988, 1994), which contains questions about people with disabilities in general, without specifying any specific disability. Given that *disability* is such a broad term, it is unknown what conceptualization of disability the respondents have in mind. This has been one of the criticisms of this scale, though it is still widely used.

Another approach uses disabilities that are specifically named, but either uses "physical disabilities" or "people with disabilities" or a specific disability for each item (e.g., "Certain jobs should be set aside for blind persons so that they don't have to compete directly with persons who do not have disabilities"; "People who have disabilities should have to pay income taxes"; Makas 1988).

A more recent scale developed by the World Health Organization (Power, Green, & WHOQOL-DIS Group, 2010) has the advantage of being validated in different languages. A review of 31 measures of attitudes toward disability (Palad et al., 2016) includes 15 that were about disability in general and determined that 23 were of usable quality. A measure of beliefs (models of disability) was used in a recent study of college students with and without disabilities (Bogart, Logan, Hospodar, & Woekel, 2019).

A very different way of assessing attitudes comes from a scale by Bogardus (1933; see also Flanagan, 1978, and Parillo & Donoghue, 2005, for updates on the scale) that was first used in the 1930s to assess attitudes toward Chinese immigrants in the United States. Following the work of Tringo (1970), I adapted the social distance scale to assess attitudes toward specific disabilities. This creates a hierarchy of acceptance for various conditions by averaging across all respondents for each condition. In this way we see relative stigma against specific disabilities compared with other disabilities. This hierarchy of acceptability has been remarkably stable over time (Olkin & Howson, 1994). Once students have researched their assigned disabilities (see Activities 3.2 and 6.4), it is a question whether their hierarchy would change to accommodate the assigned disability (see Table 11.1).

What I want to add to this discussion are other ways that one might measure changes in beliefs and attitudes toward disability. Before I give talks on disability, I often ask audience members to write on a 3 × 5 index card the one question they want to ask a person with a disability but felt they could not ask (and I do answer them after the talk). This is a useful exercise in ascertaining what people believe is permissible, intrusive, rude, or unspeakable about disability. Discussion then can be about how we negotiate social spaces with disabled people.

TABLE 11.1 SOCIAL DISTANCE SCALE FOR SPECIFIC DISABILITIES

Directions

Place an *x* in the box indicating *THE MOST INTIMATE RELATIONSHIP* that you are willing to accept with a member of each of the groups indicated.

Think of each group *AS A WHOLE*, and not the best or the worst member(s) that you have encountered.

Please provide your *FIRST* feeling reaction in each case.

Scale:
1 Would marry
2 Close kinship by marriage
3 Allow into my club
4 Would have as a personal friend
5 Live on my street as neighbors
6 Employment in my occupation
7 Citizenship in my country

Disability Type	**Level of Social Distance**						
	1	2	3	4	5	6	7
Leg brace							
Limping gait							
Amputee—one arm							
Deaf or severe hearing loss							
Blind or severe sight loss							
Amputee—one leg							
Crutches and leg brace(s)							
Paraplegic, manual wheelchair little person (dwarfism)							
Multiple sclerosis							
Facial disfigurement							
Cerebral palsy							
Quadriplegic, electric wheelchair							

TABLE 11.2 POSSIBLE EMOTIONAL RESPONSES TO CONTACT WITH A DISABLED PERSON

Scale: 1 = Not at all
2 = A little bit
3 = Moderate amount
4 = A great deal

Admiration	1	2	3	4
Pity	1	2	3	4
Awkward	1	2	3	4
Embarrassed	1	2	3	4
Inconvenienced	1	2	3	4
Anger	1	2	3	4
Inspired	1	2	3	4
Resentment	1	2	3	4

Another idea comes from a study in which respondents were asked how they felt when they encountered a person with a disability (Yuker, 1994). The emotions that were cited can be used to create a list (see Table 11.2). This requires honest reflection on the part of students and skill on the part of the instructor in holding difficult dialogues.

A further idea is to discuss the meaning of "quality of life" (QOL). There are thousands of studies using a multitude of measures of QOL. I have distilled them into a few key areas to make a short QOL measure (based on issues on QOL measures raised by Flanagan, 1978). The importance of this measure (Table 11.3) is that it elucidates the beliefs around whether QOL is significantly diminished by a disability. It would be interesting to use as a measure for the self, and then for what respondents believe would be the responses of someone with a specific kind of disability.

Table 11.4 is an assessment of able-bodied privilege. It contains a list of behaviors that a person could engage in. I have asked students to complete the first column (things they can do now) in an initial class. This raises awareness of how much nondisabled people take for granted. Then, after doing several activities over several weeks, including having been assigned a disability to "have" and to research, I ask them to fill out the second column and write or discuss in class their observations about the discrepancies in the two columns.

TABLE 11.3 OLKIN BRIEF QUALITY-OF-LIFE MEASURE.
FOR EACH OF THE AREAS LISTED BELOW, PLEASE RATE YOUR OVERALL LEVEL OF OVERALL SATISFACTION

Scale: 1 = Very dissatisfied
2 = A little dissatisfied
3 = A little satisfied
4 = Very satisfied

Items to Be Rated	**Rating Scale** *Circle One Number*			
Physical and material well-being Material well-being and financial security Health and personal safety	1	2	3	4
Relations with other people Relations with spouse Having and raising children Relations with parents, siblings, or other relatives Relations with friends	1	2	3	4
Social, community, and civic activities Activities related to helping/encouraging other people Activities relating to local and national governments	1	2	3	4
Personal development and fulfillment Intellectual development Personal understanding and planning Occupational role Creativity and personal expression	1	2	3	4
Recreation Socializing Passive and observational recreational activities Active and participatory recreational activities	1	2	3	4

TABLE 11.4 ABLE-BODIED PRIVILEGE.

PUT A CHECK NEXT TO THOSE ITEMS YOU CAN NOW DO

	You Now	You with Disability
I can arrange to be in the company of people with my level of ability most of the time with relative ease.		
If I should need to move my residence, I can be pretty sure of finding a house or apartment that will accommodate me physically.		
I can be pretty sure that my new neighbors will be neutral or pleasant to me.		
I can turn on the television or open a newspaper and see people of similar ability to me widely represented.		
I am familiar with the history of people similar to me in ability.		
I can be pretty sure of my ability to have my voice heard in a group in which I am the only person with my level of ability.		
I can do well in a challenging situation without being called a credit to my level of ability.		
I am never asked to speak for all people of my ability group.		
I can get from Point A to Point B without worrying about how I am going to get there and how much energy each option will cost me.		
I can say "I'm tired" and not be criticized for "always being tired."		
I can get inside all buildings by the main entrance where everyone else goes and will never have to go around to a "special" entrance.		
I can come and go as I please most of the time without having to move other people out of the way.		

TABLE 11.4 CONTINUED

I can blend into a crowd reasonably well.		
I can be in a place with other people without feeling like there is a neon sign over my head saying "different."		
I can draw, cut with scissors, and do an assortment of motor skill–related things without much trouble.		
I can do something ordinary or even out of the ordinary without being thought of as "brave," "courageous," "special," or "inspirational."		
I can open a door and go through it without any difficulties.		
I can go out in public without someone making a joke about me that I've heard many, many times before.		
Other people do not touch a part of my body or a device I use (e.g., glasses) without my explicit permission.		
No one refers to parts of my body as the "good" and "bad" parts.		
I can travel without worry about getting stuck somewhere with no accessible transport.		
I can get my food in a cafeteria and eat it without assistance.		
I will never be made helpless because a battery runs out.		
I am mostly at eye level with other people.		
I am rarely stared at when in public.		
No one thinks my romantic partner is my caregiver.		
It is always assumed I can speak for myself, and others don't address the people with me instead of me directly.		
I do not have to keep saying "thank you" every few minutes for the help other people provide.		
I rarely have to accept help and charity from other people.		

(continued)

TABLE 11.4 CONTINUED

It is not suggested, either implicitly or explicitly, that someone would rather be dead than be like me or that I would be better off having died.		
When I am with other people with disabilities, it causes comments and concern.		
When I go to a movie, theater, or concert, I can sit anywhere.		
I can advocate for my child at school without my ability level being blamed for my child's performance or behavior.		
I can go grocery shopping by myself, obtain what I need without assistance, see and use the credit card machines.		
I know that I am not a "token" hire or organization member.		
I am not afraid that I will be targeted as an "easy" mark for violence or assault.		
When interacting with a store employee that person does not talk to me like I'm a child, or lean down to me, or raise the register of their voice, or call me honey or sweetheart, or treat me like I'm stupid.		
I can use most over-the-counter products without worrying they will cause a painful or dangerous reaction.		
I can visit my friends' residences without difficulty.		
People do not question my ability to parent.		
When I wake up in the morning, I am fairly certain that I can do the things I planned for that day.		
I am confident that my employer and colleagues judge me by my abilities.		
I can plan my days without worrying about accommodating medications, physical therapy, or pain.		
When I have an ordinary illness like a cold, it doesn't turn into a major calamity.		

Because using only measures of explicit attitudes may be misleading, I recommend assessing implicit bias as well. A link for an implicit attitudes measure from Harvard is https://implicit.harvard.edu/implicit/takeatest.html.

Knowledge: Virtually all the activities in this book should increase knowledge in some way—about ableism, specific disabilities, social aspects of disability, laws, systemic burdens and obstacles placed on disabled people, and more. I have tended not to quiz students on knowledge as much as I have them reflect on their own learning. However, it can be very useful to ask about specific areas of knowledge that are important to clients with disabilities. However, I have given a very brief (four questions) quiz to assess if students are getting the main points (Box 11.1). This is done less for a grade than for information about whether students are doing the reading (Olkin, 2017) and tracking major concepts. Answers are d, c, d, c.

BOX 11.1 BRIEF KNOWLEDGE QUIZ

1. **Disability-affirmative therapy emphasizes**
   a. Including the partner/family in treatment.
   b. Helping the client build a positive attitude toward multiple sclerosis (MS).
   c. Affirming and accepting the negative automatic thoughts about MS.
   d. Proper incorporation of MS into the case formulation.
2. **The three major models of disability are**
   a. Moral, medical, ecosystemic.
   b. Religious, medical, ecosystemic.
   c. Moral, medical, social.
   d. Moral, ecosystemic, social.
3. **When working with a client with a disability called "quiggle," a good way to speak to them would be**
   a. "You have the 'diagnose-and-adios' disease."
   b. "I see you are a quiggle patient."
   c. "I understand you are a quiggler."
   d. "I understand you are living with quiggle."
4. **Regarding screening for depression in a new client with a disability, a good suggestion would be for the therapist to**
   a. Administer the Beck Depression Inventory as is.
   b. Administer the Beck Depression Inventory omitting two questions on fatigue.
   c. Ask about a history of depression prior to onset of the disability.
   d. Asking two specific questions about the last 2 weeks with regard to mood and interest or pleasure.

Skills: Note that the empirical literature demonstrates a weak link between attitudes and behavior (Olkin, 1999). Activity 10.6 is about doing a behavior, that is, taking affirmative action on behalf of disabled people. Skills are another type of behavior, and clinical skills that are culturally responsive toward clients with disabilities are the ultimate goal. Activity 10.7 has participants respond to clinical vignettes. This is meant as an activity but could serve as well as a pre- and posttest after other activities.

Last, I designed a questionnaire for feedback at the end of a 45-hour class on clients with disabilities (Table 11.5). Some items moved in the desired direction. Students felt less pity, were more aware of ableism and able-bodied privilege, and even reflected on their own past behaviors with people with disabilities. However, they rated lower in their ability to ask clients about their disabilities, work with a blind client, or see a client in a wheelchair. And contrary to what one might hope, they rated higher in feeling inspired by people with disabilities, that is, a stereotype of people with disabilities as inspirational for those without disabilities (a common theme in movies). Because of this feedback, I included in this book an activity using clinical vignettes (Activity 10.7) so students can practice skills. However, I used those vignettes in my class as well, so clearly students need more practice in interacting with disabled clients. Supervised role plays with people with real disabilities (not simulated) would be the ideal tool to increase skills. As all empirical literature notes, contact with people with disabilities is the most robust means of improving attitudes, but that contact should be between equals. Therapy has an inherent power dynamic that puts clients and therapists at different levels. Thus, role plays are an essential means of decreasing discomfort and increasing skills. However, the person playing the client must be disabled—using confederates is not authentic, just as it would not be for someone pretending to be gay or a person of color.

In conclusion, it is important that we assess the outcomes of any activity designed to change attitudes, knowledge, skills, or behaviors of students about or toward people with disabilities. These outcomes should be assessed both shortly following the activity and at Time 2, at least 1 week later, if not longer. Only by careful assessment can we begin to amass data that will be useful in designing optimal means to the desired outcomes. Understanding the mechanisms by which individuals change their perceptions and behaviors ultimately can allow us to think about changes on a more societal level. The final goal is to make the world a better place for people with disabilities by changing the sociopolitical and economic factors that hinder optimum living. The activities in this book are only an initial step.

TABLE 11.5 OLKIN SELF-RATING OF ATTITUDES AND SKILLS.
AS OF RIGHT NOW, I WOULD RATE MYSELF AS FOLLOWS:

Scale: 1 = Not at all true
2 = Just a very little true
3 = True
4 = Very much true

Items	Ratings			
	1	2	3	4
I feel less pity toward people with disabilities than before the class.				
I am more knowledgeable about at least three different disabilities.				
I have confidence I would know how to ask about a client's disability in session.				
I would be anxious about seeing a new client using a wheelchair.				
I know the information in the important laws relevant to people with disabilities.				
I could give the legal definition of *disability* in federal law.				
I am more aware of able-bodied privilege.				
I feel more inspired by people with disabilities than before the class.				
I have specific plans for how to make changes for people with disabilities.				
I am more able to work with a client who was blind.				
I have reflected on microaggressions I have done toward persons with disabilities in the past.				
I have a greater understanding of "ableism."				

References for Chapter 11

Bogardus, E. S. (1933). A social distance scale. *Sociology and Social Research, 22*, 265–271.

Bogart, K. R., Logan, S. W., Hospodar, C., & Woekel, E. (2019). Disability models and attitudes among college students with and without disabilities. *Stigma and Health, 4*(3), 260–263. https://doi.org/10.1037/sah0000142

Flanagan, J. C. (1978). A research approach to improving our quality of life. *American Psychologist, 33*, 138–147.

Makas, E. (1988). Positive attitudes toward disabled people: Disabled and nondisabled persons' perspectives. *Journal of Social Issues, 44*(1), 49–61.

Olkin, R. (1999). *What psychotherapists should know about disability*. New York: Guilford Press.

Olkin, R. (2017). *Disability-affirmative therapy: A case formulation template for your clients with disabilities*. New York: Oxford University Press.

Olkin, R., & Howson, L. (1994). Attitudes toward and images of physical disability. *Journal of Social Behavior and Personality, 9*(5), 81–96.

Palad, Y. Y., Barquia, R., Domingo, H., Flores, C. K., Padilla, L. I., & Ramel, J. M. (2016). Scoping review of instruments measuring attitudes toward disability. *Disability and Health Journal, 9*(3), 354–374.

Parillo, V. N., & Donoghue, C. (2005). Updating the Bogardus social distance studies: A new national survey. *Social Science Journal, 42*, 257–271.

Power, M. J., Green, A. M., & WHOQOL-DIS Group. (2010). The Attitudes to Disability Scale (ADS): Development and psychometric properties. *Journal of Intellectual Disability Research, 54*, 860–874.

Tringo, J. L. (1970). The hierarchy of preferences toward disability groups. *Journal of Special Education, 44*, 295–306.

Yuker, H. E. (Ed.). (1988). *Attitudes towards persons with disabilities*. New York: Springer.

Yuker, H. E. (1994). Variables that influence attitudes toward persons with disabilities: Conclusions from the data. *Journal of Social Behavior and Personality* [Special issue], *9*, 3–22.

Index